NOTABLE U.S. ERROR COINS 2025

200+ High-Quality Images and Expert Tips to Identify, Preserve, and Profit from Valuable Coins

ORSON KANE

TABLE OF CONTENTS

■ ■ ■ ■ ■ ■ ■ ■ ■ ■ ■ ■

INTRODUCTION..7
Introduction to the World of Error Coins 7
Why Collect Error Coins in 2024 8
What to Expect from This Book...................................10

CHAPTER 1
INTRODUCTION TO ERROR COIN COLLECTING..13
History and Appeal of U.S. Error Coins 13
Definition of Numismatics and Its
Connection to Error Coins 14
Basics of Coin Collecting: Where to Start 16
Mint Marks and Their Importance 17

CHAPTER 2
STRUCTURE AND TERMINOLOGY
OF COINS...19
Anatomy of a Coin...19
Key Terms for Error Coin Collectors 20
Coin Classification System 22

CHAPTER 3
GETTING STARTED WITH ERROR COINS............27
Essential Tools for Detecting Errors 27
How to Handle and Store Coins 29
Table: Types of Coin Storage Options and Their

Features 30
Where to Find Error Coins 31

CHAPTER 4
MAIN CATEGORIES OF COIN ERRORS 34
Minting Errors: Planchet, Strike, and Die Errors 34
Rare Errors and What Makes Them Valuable 37
Practical Approach to Identifying Subtle Errors 38

CHAPTER 5
VALUABLE ERROR COINS BY DENOMINATION ... 40
Errors on Lincoln Pennies 40
Market Values for Lincoln Penny Errors 42
Errors on Jefferson Nickels 42
Market Values for Jefferson Nickel Errors 44
Errors on Washington Quarters 44
Market Values for Washington Quarter Errors 46
Errors on Roosevelt Dimes 46
Market Values for Roosevelt Dime Errors 47

CHAPTER 6
EVALUATING AND SELLING YOUR ERROR
COINS 48
Factors Affecting Coin Values 48
Strategies for Accurate Coin Appraisal 50
Selling Options: Auctions, Coin Shows, and Private
Sales 51

CHAPTER 7
FAMOUS U.S. ERROR COINS 53
The 1955 Doubled Die Lincoln Cent: An Iconic Error 53
The 1937-D Three-Legged Buffalo Nickel:
A Visual Oddity 54

The 1942/41 Mercury Dime: A Wartime Mishap 55
The 2004 Wisconsin Extra Leaf Quarter:
A Modern Mystery 56
The 1922 No D Lincoln Cent:
A Scarcity of Mintmarks 57
Notable U.S. Error Coins: A Collector's Guide 58
Lincoln Pennies 58
Jefferson Nickels 65
Washington Quarters 72
Roosevelt Dimes 79
Additional Error Coins 85

CHAPTER 8
BUILDING A SUCCESSFUL ERROR COIN
COLLECTION 126
Diversifying Your Collection 126
Preserving Your Collection 127
Connecting with the Coin Community 129
Strategies for Long-Term Success 130

CHAPTER 9
FUTURE TRENDS IN ERROR
COIN COLLECTING 132
Technological Advances in Error Coin Detection 132
Market Trends in Error Coin Collecting 134
Fluctuations in Error Coin Values 135
The Role of Social Media and Online Marketplaces 136
The Future of Error Coin Collecting 138

CHAPTER 10
FAQS AND COMMON MYTHS ABOUT
ERROR COINS 139
Addressing Frequent Questions 139
Busting Myths and Misconceptions 142

CONCLUSION.. 145
Appendix 149
Resources for Collectors 151
Market Tables..152
Notable Error Coin Lists...153
Summary..154

YOU EXCLUSIVE BONUS....................................... 155

INTRODUCTION

■ ■ ■ ■ ■ ■ ■ ■ ■ ■ ■ ■ ■ ■ ■ ■ ■

Introduction to the World of Error Coins

Imagine holding a coin in your hand, one you might have overlooked countless times before—a penny, a nickel, or maybe a quarter. It's ordinary, seemingly unremarkable. But what if, in that small piece of metal, there was a hidden treasure? Not in the sense of gold or jewels, but something far rarer: a mistake. A rare error, the kind that could turn a simple coin into something worth much more than its face value.

Welcome to the fascinating world of error coins. This world is one where precision meets imperfection, where machinery and human oversight intertwine, creating an unexpected legacy for collectors and historians alike. These coins, which are mistakenly struck or produced by mints, reveal stories not only about the errors themselves but also about the intricate processes of coin production and the history behind them.

Error coins offer a unique glimpse into the past. They capture moments where machinery faltered or where human intervention failed to catch discrepancies. These anomalies are rare, each one unique in its imperfection. For collectors, these coins are more than currency—they are artifacts of historical significance, tangible pieces of a process that is meant to be exact but, like everything, sometimes falls short.

But the value of error coins goes beyond their historical and aesthetic appeal. Some of these errors are incredibly valuable, with prices soaring in auctions and private sales. Collectors, both novice and experienced, find themselves captivated by the possibility of discovering an error coin in their everyday change, transforming a hobby into a potential avenue for financial gain.

For many, the journey into this niche of numismatics begins with curiosity—a curiosity that eventually grows into a passion. It may start with a small find—a double-die penny or a coin struck off-center—that ignites a deeper interest. From there, collectors find themselves seeking out other anomalies, learning the language of error coins, and diving into forums, shows, and online communities to share their discoveries and knowledge.

As you embark on this journey, you'll soon realize that error coins represent the unexpected beauty of imperfection. They are a testament to how even a system designed for accuracy, like a minting process, can produce something unique and valuable when it deviates from the norm. And while many collectors start small, their fascination often leads them to explore beyond the surface, developing skills to identify, appraise, and collect these fascinating pieces of history.

This book is your guide to that world, offering you the tools, knowledge, and insights needed to not only understand error coins but to actively seek them out. Whether you're new to the hobby or a seasoned collector looking to refine your expertise, this book will provide you with the information and resources to make your journey both enjoyable and rewarding.

Why Collect Error Coins in 2024

In 2024, error coin collecting has never been more exciting or accessible. Technology and information are at our fingertips like never before, making it possible for collectors to dive deeper into the world of error coins from the comfort of their own homes. High-resolution images, online databases, and digital magnification tools allow collectors to scrutinize and identify errors with unprecedented accuracy. But why, exactly, should you start or continue collecting error coins this year?

For starters, the market for error coins is thriving. Collectors and investors alike are drawn to the potential financial rewards these coins offer. Error coins can sell for hundreds, even thousands of dollars, depending on their rarity and condition. In a time when people are looking for alternative investments and new ways to supplement their income, error coin collecting offers a tangible, intriguing, and potentially profitable option. Finding that one rare error coin in your pocket change could significantly boost your earnings—an opportunity that many enthusiasts find hard to resist.

But beyond the financial allure, 2024 is a pivotal time for the numismatic community. Interest in error coins is on the rise, partly due to the internet's role in spreading information and the ease with which collectors can now connect. Social media groups, forums, and online auctions have created a thriving community where knowledge, tips, and discoveries are shared. As collectors become more informed and more engaged, the appreciation for error coins—both for their history and their uniqueness—continues to grow.

At the same time, changes in minting technology and processes mean that while certain types of errors might become less frequent, others may emerge. Coins minted today will one day be the error coins of the future. Therefore, collectors who start now not only get the chance to explore past anomalies but also to understand and perhaps predict which errors might become valuable in the future. It's an exciting time for those who want to build their knowledge and be ahead of the curve in this evolving field.

There's also the sheer joy of the hunt. For those who appreciate history, treasure hunting, and puzzles, collecting error coins is the perfect hobby. Every coin roll becomes an opportunity, every coin show a treasure trove waiting to be explored. The satisfaction of identifying an error coin, especially one that others may have missed, is incomparable. It's not just about finding something of value; it's about the thrill of discovery, of knowing that you have the skills and knowledge to spot a rare piece among the ordinary.

Collecting error coins in 2024 also means being part of a larger community. Whether you attend local coin shows, participate in online forums, or simply enjoy cataloging your finds at home, you're joining a network of like-minded individuals who share your passion. This sense of community can be a source of knowledge, encouragement, and camaraderie, making the experience even more rewarding. The friendships and connections formed through this shared interest often extend beyond the coins themselves, creating lasting bonds.

Lastly, as the world becomes more digital, there's something inherently satisfying about collecting physical objects like coins. In a time when digital currencies and intangible assets dominate the financial landscape, holding a coin that represents history, rarity, and value offers a sense of connection to something tangible and enduring. Error coins, in particular, carry the stories of their creation—moments when technology or human oversight left its mark on the minting process. Collecting these coins is like preserving those stories, capturing them for future generations.

What to Expect from This Book

This book is designed to be your ultimate guide to the world of U.S. error coins. Whether you are a seasoned collector or just beginning your journey, it provides the information you need to identify, collect, and appreciate error coins with confidence. Structured to cater to different levels of expertise, this guide ensures that you have the tools to expand your collection and deepen your understanding of this fascinating hobby.

In the chapters that follow, you will first be introduced to the history and allure of error coins, giving you the background needed to appreciate their significance. We will explore how the U.S. Mint works, the stages in the coin production process, and where errors are most likely to occur. Understanding this process is crucial, as it forms the foundation for identifying genuine errors versus damage or wear.

Next, you'll find a detailed breakdown of the different types of error coins. From planchet errors, like clipped or wrong planchets, to die errors such as doubled dies and die cracks, each type of error will be explained with clarity. Alongside explanations, you'll see high-quality images highlighting these errors, so you know exactly what to look for when examining your coins. The goal is to make you comfortable with recognizing these anomalies, ensuring you don't miss out on valuable finds.

But identifying error coins is only part of the journey. This book will also guide you on how to handle and preserve your coins to maintain their value. You will learn best practices for using tools like magnifiers and microscopes, as well as tips for storing your collection safely. Proper care and management of your coins are essential for keeping them in their best condition and maximizing their value over time.

For those looking to monetize their collection, chapters will delve into the current market for error coins. You'll gain insights into the factors that influence a coin's value—rarity, demand, and condition—and learn how to accurately appraise your finds. The book will also cover strategies for selling error coins, including online platforms like eBay and Heritage Auctions, as well as coin shows and private sales. Armed with this knowledge, you'll be well-equipped to make informed decisions, ensuring that you get the most out of your collection.

Additionally, the book includes case studies of some of the most famous error coins in U.S. history. You'll read about the 1955 Doubled Die Lincoln Cent, the 1937-D Three-Legged Buffalo Nickel, and other significant finds that have made headlines and captivated collectors. These stories not only illustrate the value of error coins but also offer inspiration, showing that even the smallest details can turn an ordinary coin into a priceless treasure.

To make this book even more valuable, it includes practical resources such as updated lists of the most sought-after error coins by denomination and market value. You'll also find downloadable guides and video tutorials that provide step-by-step instructions for searching through your pocket change, identifying errors, and even connecting with other collectors. These additional tools aim to make your collecting experience more engaging and rewarding, ensuring that you have all the support needed to succeed.

By the time you finish this book, you will have developed a thorough understanding of error coins and the skills needed to identify and collect them effectively. You'll gain confidence in your ability to spot valuable finds, and you'll be better prepared to navigate the world of numismatics, whether as a casual hobbyist or a serious collector. The thrill of discovering rare coins and the potential financial rewards are within your reach. Let's start this journey together—one coin, one discovery at a time.

CHAPTER 1
INTRODUCTION TO ERROR COIN COLLECTING

■ ■ ■ ■ ■ ■ ■ ■ ■ ■ ■ ■ ■ ■ ■

History and Appeal of U.S. Error Coins

The history of U.S. error coins is as intriguing as the coins themselves. To truly appreciate them, one must first understand the broader history of coin production in the United States. Since the establishment of the U.S. Mint in 1792, millions of coins have been struck every year, each one intended to be a perfect representation of its denomination. Yet, despite the advanced machinery and strict quality control processes, errors occasionally slip through, creating coins that defy expectations and, in some cases, significantly increase in value.

Error coins have long fascinated collectors and numismatists alike. They serve as physical evidence of the complex and often imperfect minting process. Early error coins were considered little more than factory defects, with little attention given to them beyond their nominal value. However, as the numismatic community grew and collectors began to appreciate the uniqueness and rarity of these errors, attitudes shifted. These coins, once dismissed as flawed, became valuable and sought-after objects of fascination.

The appeal of error coins lies in their rarity and uniqueness. Unlike regular coins, which are produced in vast quantities, error coins are accidents—unexpected anomalies in the production line. This means that each error coin is one-of-a-kind, representing a moment where something went wrong, and the usual standards of production were not met. For collectors, this is what makes error coins so special. They are tangible remnants of the minting process, showing how even the most precise systems can falter.

Over the decades, certain error coins have risen to legendary status. The 1955 Doubled Die Lincoln Cent, for example, is one of the most famous and valuable error coins in U.S. history. Its doubling effect, where the date and inscription appear as if shadowed, was caused by a misalignment during the die production process. When collectors began to notice this error, the coin's value skyrocketed, turning what was once a common penny into a sought-after treasure. Such coins capture the imagination of collectors and numismatists, showing that sometimes, even a simple mistake can create something extraordinary.

The appeal of U.S. error coins extends beyond their rarity; it taps into the thrill of discovery. For many collectors, finding an error coin in pocket change or during a coin roll hunt is a moment of pure excitement. It's not just about the potential financial gain—though that's certainly part of it—but also about the sense of connection to history and the feeling of holding a rare, tangible piece of that history. Error coins are not only objects of beauty and intrigue; they are artifacts that tell stories of how they came to be. This, for many, is the true appeal.

Definition of Numismatics and Its Connection to Error Coins

Numismatics is the study or collection of currency, including coins, tokens, paper money, and related objects. While it encompasses the entire world of currency, from ancient coins to modern banknotes, error coins hold a special place within the field. For numismatists, error coins are fascinating anomalies that reveal the intricacies and challenges of minting processes. They represent an intersection between art, history, and technology, each one offering insight into the time and method of its production.

Error coins often become the focal point for many numismatists because they embody the very essence of numismatics—an exploration of currency that goes beyond face value. Unlike typical coins, which adhere to strict standards, error coins deviate from these norms, making them a subject of detailed study. The numismatist examines these deviations, understanding not only what went wrong but why it happened. It's a pursuit that requires keen observation, historical knowledge, and sometimes, a bit of detective work.

The connection between numismatics and error coins is also rooted in the value that these anomalies can bring. Numismatists often see error coins as opportunities, both for education and for investment. Studying an error coin can reveal details about the minting process and the evolution of coin design over time. For example, die varieties—where minor differences appear in coins struck by different dies—can illustrate changes in mint technology or production methods over the years.

In addition to the educational aspect, error coins represent a lucrative niche within the numismatic market. Coins that display rare or significant errors, such as off-center strikes, die breaks, or double dies, can fetch impressive sums among collectors. For this reason, many numismatists focus on error coins as a way to combine their passion for currency with an investment strategy. The right find can turn a modest collection into a valuable portfolio.

Numismatics, at its core, is about uncovering stories through currency. Error coins provide a unique opportunity for this, as each one tells a story of a mistake that somehow made it into circulation. They are tangible evidence of history's surprises, and for numismatists, they offer endless possibilities for discovery, research, and understanding.

Basics of Coin Collecting: Where to Start

For anyone interested in diving into the world of error coins, the basics of coin collecting provide a strong foundation. Beginning collectors often feel overwhelmed by the sheer variety of coins and the knowledge required to identify and appraise them. However, starting with error coins can be an exciting and manageable way to enter the hobby, as these coins offer a specific focus and a clear path for exploration.

The first step in coin collecting, especially for error coins, is to familiarize yourself with basic numismatic tools and resources. A magnifying glass or, better yet, a digital microscope, is essential for examining coins closely. Errors are often subtle, requiring careful inspection to identify, so having the right tools is crucial. Additionally, building a small library of reference books, such as the *Red Book* (A Guide Book of United States Coins) and specialized error coin guides, will provide valuable information on what to look for and how to identify various errors.

Next, it's important to start small and local. Begin by examining the coins you come across in daily life—pocket change, coin rolls from banks, or even coins passed down from family members. This approach allows you to practice identifying errors without making any financial investment. Many collectors have found valuable error coins just by being vigilant with the coins they handle every day.

Coin roll hunting is another popular way to start collecting error coins. This involves purchasing rolls of coins from banks and sorting through them for errors or rare varieties. It's an inexpensive and exciting way to engage with the hobby, as you never know what treasures might be waiting in a roll of seemingly ordinary coins. Coin roll hunting also helps beginners develop their skills in identifying errors and understanding the subtle differences that distinguish a genuine error from common wear and tear.

Once you've gained some experience with coins from circulation, you can expand your search to coin shops, shows, and online marketplaces like eBay or specialized numismatic auction sites. These platforms offer a wider variety of error coins, and you'll encounter coins from different periods and mints, allowing you to deepen your expertise. However, it's important to be cautious when purchasing coins, as the market for error coins can sometimes attract counterfeiters and sellers who misrepresent coins. Building relationships with reputable dealers and consulting reference materials are essential steps in protecting yourself and your collection.

Storage and preservation are critical aspects of coin collecting, especially for error coins, which can be more valuable than regular coins due to their rarity. Proper handling is key; using gloves or holding coins by their edges prevents oils and dirt from damaging the coin's surface. Coins should be stored in protective holders like Mylar flips or airtight capsules to prevent exposure to air, moisture, and contaminants. A well-preserved error coin retains its value, and proper care ensures that your collection remains in the best possible condition over time.

Mint Marks and Their Importance

Mint marks are small letters or symbols on coins that indicate the mint where the coin was produced. In the United States, these marks are crucial for collectors, as they help identify the origin of the coin and sometimes even its value. Error coin collectors, in particular, must pay close attention to mint marks because certain mints are associated with specific types of errors, and identifying these can be the key to unlocking the story behind an error coin.

The U.S. Mint has several facilities across the country, each producing different denominations and quantities of coins. The primary mints include Philadelphia (no mint mark or "P"), Denver ("D"), San Francisco ("S"), and West Point ("W"). In the past, other mints like Carson City ("CC") and New Orleans ("O") also operated. Each mint's mark is a clue that numismatists use to trace a coin's origin. For example, a coin with a "D" mint mark was produced in Denver, while one with an "S" was struck in San Francisco. The absence of a mint mark typically indicates Philadelphia.

For error coin collectors, the mint mark is more than just a letter. Certain mints have a history of producing specific errors or are known for minting smaller quantities of coins. For example, coins from the San Francisco Mint often feature unique errors due to its smaller production runs and specialized minting processes. Understanding the history of each mint and the types of errors associated with them can help collectors identify and authenticate error coins more accurately.

Mint marks can also influence a coin's rarity and value. A coin produced at a less common mint may be worth more, particularly if it features an error. For instance, a doubled die error on a coin with a rare mint mark can significantly increase its value, as it becomes an even rarer anomaly. Collectors who pay attention to mint marks have an advantage when searching for error coins, as they can quickly identify and assess the significance of a coin based on this small but crucial detail.

The placement and style of mint marks have changed over the years, and these changes are also important for error coin collectors. Earlier mint marks were often hand-punched into dies, leading to variations like repunched mint marks (RPMs), where the mint mark appears doubled or misplaced. These errors, while subtle, are valuable to collectors who seek out these distinctive features. Similarly, changes in mint mark placement or design can reveal important information about the era in which a coin was produced, helping collectors trace its history and authenticity.

In summary, mint marks are an integral part of understanding and collecting error coins. They provide insight into the coin's origin, its minting history, and its potential value. For collectors, recognizing and interpreting mint marks can be the difference between discovering a valuable piece of history or overlooking a hidden treasure. As you build your collection, paying attention to these small details will become second nature, enhancing both your expertise and your enjoyment of this fascinating hobby.

CHAPTER 2
STRUCTURE AND TERMINOLOGY OF COINS

■ ■ ■ ■ ■ ■ ■ ■ ■ ■ ■ ■ ■ ■ ■ ■ ■ ■

Anatomy of a Coin

To understand error coins thoroughly, it's essential to first become familiar with the anatomy of a coin. Each part of a coin carries specific information, and understanding these parts helps collectors identify errors accurately. At its core, a coin consists of three primary components: the obverse, the reverse, and the edge. Additionally, it features various inscriptions, mint marks, and design elements that can help identify errors when they are not as intended.

1. Obverse:

The obverse is the "heads" side of the coin. It typically features a portrait or emblem, such as the image of a historical figure (e.g., Abraham Lincoln on the penny). This side often contains important elements like the date, mint mark, and mottoes such as "In God We Trust." For error coin collectors, the obverse is crucial as it can reveal common errors like die cracks, double dies, or off-center strikes.

2. Reverse:

The reverse is the "tails" side of the coin. It usually features a design representing something symbolic (e.g., the Lincoln Memorial on the penny or an eagle on older quarters). Like the obverse, the reverse can contain errors such as misaligned dies, which cause a partial or shifted design.

3. **Edge**:

The edge of the coin may be plain, reeded (with raised ridges), or engraved with lettering (like the edge of the Presidential dollar coins). Errors on the edge can include missing reeding or the appearance of an incorrectly applied edge inscription. Edge errors are particularly interesting because they often occur when a coin is struck outside its retaining collar, resulting in broadstrikes or partial collars.

4. **Rim**:

The rim is the raised outer edge of a coin that serves as a boundary for the obverse and reverse designs. Errors in the rim can include cuds, which are raised lumps caused by a break in the die.

5. **Field**:

The flat area between the raised elements of the design (such as the portrait and inscriptions) is called the field. It is prone to errors like die clashes, where the imprint of the obverse and reverse dies overlap, creating faint, mirrored images of the design elements.

The anatomy of a coin forms the basis for identifying and categorizing errors. Familiarizing yourself with these components and their common features is the first step to recognizing anomalies that may indicate valuable error coins.

Key Terms for Error Coin Collectors

Understanding key terminology is crucial for anyone serious about collecting and identifying error coins. Each term describes a specific type of error or characteristic, which can significantly influence a coin's value and rarity. Below is a list of essential terms for error coin collectors, along with definitions and examples:

Planchet: The blank piece of metal on which a coin design is stamped. Planchet errors, such as clipped planchets, occur when the blank is improperly cut, resulting in a coin with a missing portion.

Die: The engraved stamp used to impress the design onto the planchet. Errors associated with dies include:

1. **Double Die**: An error where the die is misaligned during its preparation, causing the design to appear doubled on the coin.

2. **Die Crack**: A flaw where the die develops a crack, creating raised lines on the surface of the coin.

Strike: The process of stamping the planchet with the die. Errors related to the strike include:

1. **Off-Center Strike**: Occurs when the coin is not properly centered under the die, resulting in a partial design.

2. **Broadstrike**: Happens when the coin is struck without a collar, causing it to expand beyond its usual diameter.

3. **Cud**: A raised, irregular area on the rim of a coin caused by a piece of the die breaking off during the striking process.

4. **Mint Mark**: A small letter indicating the mint where the coin was produced (e.g., "D" for Denver, "S" for San Francisco). Errors related to mint marks include **repunched mint marks (RPM)**, where the mint mark appears twice due to being stamped in slightly different locations.

5. **Hub**: The tool used to create dies. If the hub misaligns during production, it can cause errors like the double die.

6. **Reeding**: The raised ridges on the edge of some coins. Missing reeding is a notable edge error, often occurring when a coin is struck outside the retaining collar.

7. **Collar**: A device that surrounds the planchet during striking, controlling its size and shape. Errors involving the collar include **partial collar errors**, where only part of the coin's edge is reeded.

8. **Clash Marks**: When the obverse and reverse dies come together without a planchet in place, they strike each other, leaving faint impressions of their designs on each other.

9. **Cameo Effect**: Not an error, but a desirable effect where the coin's design appears frosted, contrasting with the polished field. It's often sought after in proof coins.

These terms form the vocabulary of error coin collecting. Knowing them and their implications can help collectors better understand the types of errors they encounter and how those errors affect a coin's value.

Coin Classification System

Coins are not all created equal, and the numismatic community has developed a classification system to evaluate coins based on their condition, rarity, and errors. For error coins, understanding this system is vital, as it directly impacts the coin's market value. The three main components of coin classification are grading, rarity, and error type.

1. Grading Coins

Grading is the process of assessing a coin's condition, which ranges from Poor (P-1) to Mint State (MS-70). The more pristine a coin, the higher its grade. Coin grades are typically determined by experts using a grading scale developed by organizations like the Professional Coin Grading Service (PCGS) or Numismatic Guaranty Corporation (NGC).

GRADE	DESCRIPTION
Poor (P-1)	Barely identifiable; heavily worn.
Good (G-4)	Major features visible but significantly worn.
Fine (F-12)	Moderate wear; all major details are clear.
Very Fine (VF-20)	Light wear; most details remain distinct.
Extremely Fine (EF-40)	Minimal wear; sharp details and clear fields.
About Uncirculated (AU-50)	Slight wear visible on the highest points.
Mint State (MS-60 to MS-70)	No wear; sharp details and flawless surface.

The grading table helps numismatists standardize evaluations, ensuring consistent assessments across the market. For error coins, a higher grade significantly increases value, as errors on well-preserved coins are rarer and thus more desirable.

2. Rarity

Rarity plays a significant role in determining a coin's value, especially for error coins. Error coins are often classified into categories based on their frequency:

RARITY SCALE	DESCRIPTION
Common	Errors frequently encountered (e.g., minor die cracks).
Scarce	Errors that occur less often but are not rare (e.g., off-center strikes).
Rare	Errors with few known examples (e.g., broadstrikes on silver dollars).
Very Rare	Errors that occur only once or a few times (e.g., wrong planchet errors on high-denomination coins).

Understanding rarity helps collectors prioritize their searches and investments. While common errors are accessible and a good starting point, rare and very rare errors are usually the focus of serious collectors aiming to build a high-value collection.

3. Error Type Classification

Error coins are categorized based on the type of error that occurred during production. These categories help collectors understand the nature of the mistake and how it affects the coin's appearance and value. Below is a breakdown of common error types:

Planchet Errors: These occur when there is a problem with the blank coin before it is struck. Examples include:

- **Clipped Planchet**: A coin with a portion missing due to an incomplete punch.
- **Lamination Error**: A flaw in the metal composition causing a peeling effect on the coin's surface.

Die Errors: Errors involving the dies used to strike coins. Examples include:

- **Double Die**: The most famous and valuable error type, where the design is doubled due to a misaligned die during preparation.
- **Die Clash**: Occurs when the dies strike each other without a planchet in place, leaving faint impressions of one die on the other.

Strike Errors: Errors occurring during the striking process. Examples include:

- **Off-Center Strike**: The coin is struck off-center, leaving part of the design missing.
- **Broadstrike**: A coin struck without a collar, causing it to spread out beyond its usual dimensions.

Edge Errors: These errors occur on the edge of the coin, such as:

- **Partial Collar**: The collar only partially engages with the coin, resulting in an uneven edge.
- **Missing Reeded Edge**: Coins that are supposed to have ridges on their edge but lack them due to striking outside the collar.

ERROR TYPE	EXAMPLE	DESCRIPTION
Planchet Errors	Clipped Planchet	A coin missing a piece due to improper blank cutting.
Die Errors	Double Die	A coin with a doubled design due to die misalignment.
Strike Errors	Off-Center Strike	A coin struck off-center, showing a partial design.
Edge Errors	Missing Reeded Edge	An error where the coin's edge lacks the expected reeding.

Understanding these categories allows collectors to quickly identify and classify errors they encounter. Each error type has its own market, with some, like double dies and broadstrikes, being more valuable due to their rarity and visual impact.

By learning the anatomy of a coin, familiarizing oneself with the key terminology, and understanding the classification system, collectors lay the groundwork for success in the world of error coin collecting. Each step is part of a comprehensive approach that combines knowledge, observation, and practical application, enabling collectors to identify valuable coins and build impressive collections.

As you progress in this journey, this foundational knowledge will become an indispensable tool, helping you make informed decisions, spot rarities, and appreciate the fascinating nuances of error coins.

CHAPTER 3

GETTING STARTED WITH ERROR COINS

■ ■ ■ ■ ■ ■ ■ ■ ■ ■ ■ ■ ■ ■ ■ ■ ■

Essential Tools for Detecting Errors

The journey into error coin collecting begins with the right tools. While the thrill of discovering a valuable error coin is exhilarating, identifying these treasures requires precision and attention to detail. Whether you're searching through your pocket change or rolls from the bank, having the proper equipment will enhance your ability to detect errors that might be hidden in plain sight.

One of the most essential tools for any coin collector is a magnifying glass or loupe. These tools allow you to closely examine the finer details of a coin, revealing subtle errors like die cracks, doubling, or planchet flaws. The ideal magnification for detecting errors is between 10x and 20x, providing a clear and detailed view of the coin without distortion. A loupe is especially helpful for portable use, fitting easily into a pocket or carrying case, making it convenient for coin shows or casual searches.

For more advanced detection, a digital microscope can be invaluable. These microscopes connect to a computer or smartphone, providing high-resolution images that can be magnified far beyond the capacity of a handheld loupe. They allow collectors to capture and analyze images, making it easier to compare coins or consult with other collectors online. Digital microscopes are particularly useful when looking for subtle errors like repunched mint marks

(RPMs) or small die breaks, where high magnification and clarity are essential.

Another must-have tool is a good light source. Proper lighting, especially with adjustable intensity, is crucial for spotting surface errors and inconsistencies. A daylight LED lamp is recommended, as it provides bright, even lighting without the yellow tint common in standard bulbs. This allows you to see the true color and texture of the coin's surface, making it easier to identify abnormalities. The right lighting setup is particularly important when inspecting fields for signs of die wear or clash marks.

A scale and calipers are also important tools, especially for identifying planchet errors. Coins with wrong planchets or incorrect weights are valuable, but these errors are often impossible to detect without precise measurement tools. A digital scale can help determine if a coin's weight falls within the expected range for its denomination. Calipers, on the other hand, measure the coin's diameter and thickness, helping to confirm whether it matches the specifications for its type.

Once you've acquired the basic tools for detecting errors, consider adding reference materials to your collection. Books like *The Official Red Book* (A Guide Book of United States Coins) and specialized guides for error coins are essential for understanding the types of errors and their potential value. Online resources and apps can also help, providing up-to-date information and images that you can use to compare your finds. A comprehensive library of references, both physical and digital, is a powerful tool for any serious error coin collector.

Lastly, invest in storage supplies that protect your tools and coins. A sturdy storage case for your equipment keeps everything organized and easily accessible, while holders like Mylar flips or coin capsules help preserve the coins you find. Proper storage ensures that both your tools and your collection remain in good condition, ready for any discovery.

How to Handle and Store Coins

Handling and storing coins properly is critical to maintaining their value and condition, especially for error coins. Even a small amount of dirt, oil, or wear can significantly reduce a coin's grade, which in turn affects its market value. Developing good habits when handling and storing your collection will protect your coins and help you build a collection that maintains its quality over time.

The first rule when handling coins is to use gloves, preferably cotton or nitrile gloves, to avoid transferring oils from your skin onto the coin's surface. Even the smallest amount of oil can lead to corrosion or discoloration over time. Alternatively, if gloves are unavailable, you should always hold coins by the edges to minimize contact with the obverse and reverse surfaces. This simple practice prevents accidental smudges or scratches that can devalue the coin.

When inspecting coins, use a clean, soft surface like a velvet pad or microfiber cloth. Placing coins on a hard or abrasive surface increases the risk of scratching or denting, particularly when using tools like loupes or digital microscopes. A soft surface provides cushioning, ensuring that your coins are protected during examination.

Storage is equally important in preserving the value of your collection. Error coins should be stored in individual holders to prevent them from touching each other. Options like Mylar flips, airtight capsules, and plastic holders are designed to protect coins from air, moisture, and handling. Airtight capsules, in particular, are excellent for high-value error coins, as they create a sealed environment that reduces exposure to environmental factors that could cause tarnish or degradation.

Table: Types of Coin Storage Options and Their Features

STORAGE OPTION	PROTECTION LEVEL	FEATURES	RECOMMENDED USE
Mylar Flips	Medium	Inexpensive; transparent for easy viewing	Good for sorting and temporary storage
Airtight Capsules	High	Sealed environment; clear, hard plastic	Best for valuable error coins
Plastic Holders	High	Rigid structure; various sizes available	Suitable for long-term storage
Coin Albums	Medium	Organizes coins by denomination/year	Good for beginners and general collections

Error coins are particularly susceptible to environmental damage, so storing them in a controlled environment is essential. Coins should be kept away from direct sunlight, as exposure to ultraviolet (UV) light can alter their color. Similarly, storing coins in a temperature and humidity-controlled space, such as a safe or cabinet, protects them from corrosion. If you live in an area with high humidity, consider using silica gel packs within your storage cases to absorb excess moisture.

For valuable coins, certification and encapsulation may be a worthwhile investment. Professional grading services like the Professional Coin Grading Service (PCGS) or Numismatic Guaranty Corporation (NGC) can authenticate, grade, and encapsulate your error coins in tamper-evident holders. These services not only provide a professional assessment of your coin's grade but also offer a guarantee of authenticity, which can enhance the coin's value when selling or trading.

By developing proper handling techniques and investing in suitable storage options, you can preserve the integrity and value of your error coin collection. A well-preserved collection not only enhances your enjoyment as a collector but also protects your investment over time.

Where to Find Error Coins

Finding error coins is an exciting part of the collecting journey, and knowing where to look is essential for building a valuable collection. Error coins can be found in various places, from everyday pocket change to specialized coin shows. Each source offers unique opportunities and challenges, so understanding the best approaches for each setting is key to maximizing your success.

1. **Pocket Change** One of the simplest ways to start searching for error coins is by examining your pocket change. Every coin that passes through your hands is a potential treasure waiting to be discovered. Common errors, such as off-center strikes, die cracks, and double dies, can sometimes be found in circulation. This method is cost-effective and convenient, making it an ideal starting point for beginners. To increase your chances, focus on examining older coins or those that appear different from the rest. Pay attention to small details like the alignment of the design, the clarity of the inscriptions, and the appearance of the mint mark. Over time, your eye will become trained to spot subtle inconsistencies that may indicate a valuable error.

2. **Coin Roll Hunting** Coin roll hunting involves purchasing rolls of coins from banks and systematically searching through them for errors. This method offers the advantage of volume; you can examine hundreds or even thousands of coins in one session, increasing your chances of finding errors. It's particularly effective for locating **common errors**, such as off-center strikes or minor die cracks, which might be missed in everyday transactions. When engaging in coin roll hunting, it's important to establish

a process. Have your tools—such as a loupe, digital microscope, and scale—ready, and work in a well-lit area with a soft surface to protect your coins. Focus on each coin individually, inspecting both the obverse and reverse sides as well as the edge. Look for abnormalities in the design, such as doubled images, misaligned dies, or incomplete reeding. Coin roll hunting is also a great way to familiarize yourself with various coin types, mint marks, and dates, building your knowledge base. While not every roll will contain errors, persistence often pays off. Many experienced collectors have found rare errors through consistent coin roll hunting, turning inexpensive rolls into valuable finds.

3. **Local Coin Shows and Shops** Coin shows and shops are excellent places to find error coins, especially if you're looking for specific types of errors or rare varieties. Dealers at these venues often specialize in numismatics, and you'll have the opportunity to browse through a wide selection of coins, sometimes with expert guidance. Coin shows also provide a chance to connect with other collectors, share tips, and learn more about the types of errors that might be prevalent in your area. At coin shops and shows, always bring your tools and a reference guide to help evaluate potential finds. Dealers may allow you to examine coins closely before making a purchase, so take advantage of the opportunity to inspect for errors like repunched mint marks, die clashes, or planchet flaws. Be cautious and do your research; while most dealers are reputable, it's important to ensure you're getting what you pay for, especially when dealing with higher-value error coins.

4. **Online Marketplaces** The digital age has opened up new avenues for error coin collecting. Platforms like **eBay**, **Heritage Auctions**, and **Facebook groups** dedicated to numismatics allow collectors to buy and sell error coins from around the world. These online marketplaces are convenient and provide access to a broader range of error coins than you might find locally. However, caution is required when purchasing error coins online. Not all sellers are reputable, and some coins may

be misrepresented. Always check seller ratings and reviews, and consult the coin's images and descriptions carefully. Look for clear, high-resolution photos that show all parts of the coin, including the obverse, reverse, and edge. When possible, ask the seller for additional information or close-up images of potential error areas. Auction sites, like Heritage Auctions, often provide authentication and grading services, giving you peace of mind when making high-value purchases. These platforms also allow you to set budgets and bid strategically, increasing your chances of securing valuable error coins at reasonable prices.

5. **Banks and Credit Unions** For a more targeted approach, consider visiting local banks and credit unions to request bulk coin rolls. Banks often have large quantities of coins that have not yet been inspected, offering you a prime opportunity to search for errors. This method is especially effective for hunting for older denominations or special mint issues that might still be in circulation. When obtaining coin rolls from banks, be polite and respectful. Establishing a friendly relationship with bank tellers can sometimes lead to tips or access to coins that might not be readily available to others. While not every trip will yield results, consistent effort and building rapport can pay off over time, providing you with a steady stream of coins to inspect.

By exploring these various sources—pocket change, coin roll hunting, local shops, online platforms, and banks—you can maximize your chances of finding valuable error coins. Each method offers unique opportunities and experiences, and the more diverse your approach, the greater your potential for discovery. Remember, patience and persistence are key in error coin collecting. With the right tools, knowledge, and a strategic approach, you'll be well on your way to building a successful and rewarding collection.

CHAPTER 4
MAIN CATEGORIES OF COIN ERRORS

■ ■ ■ ■ ■ ■ ■ ■ ■ ■ ■ ■ ■ ■ ■ ■

The world of error coins is vast, with each type of error offering its own intrigue and value. Understanding the main categories of minting errors—planchet, strike, and die errors—provides the foundation for any collector seeking to identify and evaluate these coins. Some errors are more common, while others are extremely rare and valuable. In this chapter, we will explore the most common and rare minting errors, discussing their origins and how they impact a coin's value. Additionally, a practical approach to identifying subtle errors will be provided, equipping you with the skills to spot valuable finds.

Minting Errors: Planchet, Strike, and Die Errors

Error coins occur when something goes wrong during the minting process. This process typically involves several steps: the preparation of the planchet (the blank metal disk), the creation of the die (the tool used to stamp the coin's design), and the striking of the planchet with the die to produce the final coin. Errors can occur at any of these stages, resulting in coins with varying degrees of flaws.

Planchet Errors Planchet errors arise from issues with the blank metal disks before they are struck. These errors are relatively common but can still be valuable depending on their visibility and uniqueness. Common planchet errors include:

*   **Clipped Planchets**: A clipped planchet is missing a portion of

its edge, usually due to a misaligned cutting process when the blanks are prepared. These coins may appear crescent-shaped, with a distinct, smooth clip. While not exceedingly rare, the value of a clipped planchet coin increases if it is well-preserved and the clip is clean and clearly visible.

- **Lamination Errors**: These errors occur when a defect in the metal causes a layer of the coin's surface to peel away. Lamination errors can vary greatly in appearance, ranging from small, subtle flakes to large, prominent pieces that dramatically alter the coin's surface. The severity of the lamination and its impact on the coin's overall design determine its value.

- **Wrong Planchet Errors**: Among the more valuable planchet errors are those where a coin is struck on a planchet meant for another denomination or metal composition. Examples include a penny struck on a dime planchet or a coin struck on a foreign blank. These coins are rare because they require multiple missteps during the minting process, making them highly desirable to collectors.

Strike Errors Strike errors occur during the process of stamping the coin with the die. These errors are often visually striking, making them some of the most popular among collectors. The following are the most common types of strike errors:

- **Off-Center Strikes**: When a planchet is not properly aligned beneath the die, the resulting coin may display an off-center image, with part of the design missing. The degree of off-center strike significantly affects the coin's value. Coins that are misaligned by more than 50% while still showing the date and key design elements are particularly sought after.

- **Broadstrikes**: A broadstrike happens when the collar (the device that holds the coin in place during striking) malfunctions or is absent. This allows the coin to spread beyond its normal diameter, resulting in a coin with a larger, flatter appearance. Broadstrikes can occur with any denomination and are valued for their distinct shape and visual appeal.

- **Double Strikes and Multiple Strikes**: Sometimes, a planchet is struck more than once due to a malfunction in the minting machinery. These coins may show overlapping designs or multiple impressions of the same image, creating a dramatic effect. Double strikes are more common, while coins struck three or more times are much rarer and, consequently, more valuable.

- **Flip-Over Double Strikes**: This type of error occurs when a coin is struck, flipped over, and then struck again on the opposite side. These coins display design elements on both sides that are not in their usual orientation, creating a visually intriguing effect. Flip-over double strikes are rare and can be valuable depending on the clarity and placement of the impressions.

Die Errors Die errors result from issues with the dies used to stamp the coins. These errors can vary from minor to dramatic, and their impact on a coin's value depends on their rarity and visual appeal. Common die errors include:

- **Die Cracks**: Over time, dies can develop cracks due to the immense pressure they endure. These cracks appear as raised lines on the coin's surface, following the pattern of the die's fracture. Die cracks are generally not highly valuable unless they are large or form interesting shapes, such as connecting significant elements of the design.

- **Cuds**: A cud is a raised, blank area on a coin's surface caused by a die break. When a part of the die chips away, it leaves a void that shows up as a lump or blob on the coin. Cuds are more valuable when they appear prominently and affect a significant portion of the coin.

- **Double Dies**: Double die errors occur when the die itself is impressed with the design more than once, but in slightly different positions. Coins struck with these dies show doubled elements, such as numbers, letters, or other design features. The 1955 Doubled Die Lincoln Cent is a famous example, known for its dramatic doubling effect. Double die errors are highly sought after due to their visual distinctiveness and rarity.

- **Die Clashes**: A die clash happens when the obverse and re-verse dies strike each other without a planchet in between. This contact leaves faint, mirrored impressions of each die's design on the other, which are then transferred to coins struck afterward. Coins with die clashes show ghostly images of the opposing side's design, creating a unique appearance that can be valuable if the clash is prominent.

Rare Errors and What Makes Them Valuable

While many error coins are relatively common and easy to find, some errors are exceptionally rare. These rare errors often command high prices at auctions and are highly coveted by collectors. Several factors contribute to the value of these rare errors, including the difficulty of their creation, the visual impact of the error, and the coin's condition.

Wrong Planchet Errors are among the most valuable because they require multiple failures during the minting process. For example, a copper penny struck on a dime planchet is a rare find, as it suggests that two different denominations' planchets were mixed during production. These coins are worth significantly more than their face value, especially if they are in mint condition.

Dramatic Double Dies are also highly valued due to their rarity and the striking visual effect they produce. Coins like the 1955 Doubled Die Lincoln Cent showcase a clear doubling of the design, making them instantly recognizable and desirable. Double dies that show significant doubling of key elements, such as the date or inscriptions, are especially sought after and can sell for thousands of dollars depending on their condition and visibility.

Mule Errors, which occur when two dies from different coin types are used to strike a coin, are extremely rare and highly valuable. For example, if a coin has the obverse of a penny and the reverse of a dime, it would be considered a mule error. These errors are almost always the result of significant oversight at the mint, making them exceptionally rare and often fetching high prices among collectors.

Overstrikes and Flip-Over Strikes are also prized for their rarity and the complexity involved in their creation. These coins show multiple impressions or designs that are misaligned or flipped, creating a chaotic and visually engaging result. Collectors value these coins for their unique appearance and the challenge of understanding how they came to be.

The value of rare errors is also influenced by market demand and historical significance. Coins from specific years or mints with known error histories can become iconic, with collectors eagerly seeking out these pieces to complete their collections. The more dramatic and distinct the error, the higher the likelihood of it becoming a valuable and sought-after item in the numismatic community.

Practical Approach to Identifying Subtle Errors

Not all errors are dramatic or immediately obvious. Some are subtle and require careful observation and knowledge to identify. As an error coin collector, developing a practical approach to finding these subtle errors can help you uncover hidden treasures that others may overlook.

The first step in identifying subtle errors is to study known examples. Familiarize yourself with images of coins that feature specific errors, such as die cracks, repunched mint marks, or minor off-center strikes. Reference materials, such as books and online guides, often provide detailed images that show what these errors look like. By studying these examples, you will learn to recognize the telltale signs of subtle anomalies.

When examining coins, always use the right tools. A loupe with 10x magnification or a digital microscope can reveal small details that are not visible to the naked eye. Inspect both the obverse and reverse sides of the coin, as well as the edge, for signs of inconsistency. For example, a coin with a minor off-center strike may only show a slight shift in the design, which could be missed without magnification.

Lighting is another crucial factor. Use a daylight lamp or LED light to illuminate the coin from different angles, highlighting inconsistencies or irregularities on the surface. A slight rotation of the coin under bright light can make small cracks, doubling, or surface anomalies more visible.

Understanding the common areas for errors can also improve your chances of finding subtle errors. Mint marks, dates, and inscriptions are frequent sites for doubling or repunching errors. Pay close attention to these elements, comparing them to other coins of the same type and year. If you notice any variations, such as a doubling effect or misalignment, it could be a sign of a valuable error.

Patience and persistence are essential. Not every coin will yield an error, and the process of finding subtle anomalies can be time-consuming. However, the reward of discovering an overlooked error coin is worth the effort. By developing a systematic approach, using the right tools, and becoming familiar with what to look for, you will enhance your ability to identify subtle errors and build a more valuable collection.

Subtle errors can sometimes be the most rewarding, as they often go unnoticed by casual collectors. Those who take the time to develop their skills in detecting these nuances often find hidden gems that can significantly enhance the value of their collections. By approaching error coin hunting with a keen eye and a well-prepared toolkit, you position yourself to uncover the full spectrum of possibilities that the world of error coins has to offer.

CHAPTER 5

VALUABLE ERROR COINS BY DENOMINATION

■ ■ ■ ■ ■ ■ ■ ■ ■ ■ ■ ■ ■ ■ ■ ■ ■

Understanding the value and types of errors in U.S. coins involves exploring each denomination and identifying the most notable and valuable mistakes. This chapter delves into the common and rare errors associated with Lincoln Pennies, Jefferson Nickels, Washington Quarters, and Roosevelt Dimes, offering detailed insights into why these errors occur and what makes them valuable. Market value tables will provide a practical guide to understanding the financial potential of these coins.

Errors on Lincoln Pennies

The Lincoln Penny, in circulation since 1909, is one of the most commonly collected coins. Due to its long history and frequent design changes, it has produced many error varieties, making it a cornerstone for error coin enthusiasts.

One of the most iconic errors in U.S. numismatics is the 1955 Doubled Die Lincoln Cent. This coin became famous for its striking doubling on the obverse, particularly in the date and inscriptions like "LIBERTY." The doubling effect is so prominent that it's easily visible without magnification, making it a collector's dream. What caused this error was a misalignment during the die production process, where the design was impressed onto the die twice but not perfectly aligned. This error significantly impacted the coin's value. In high grades, particularly uncirculated ones, these coins can fetch tens of thousands of dollars. Even in lower grades, the 1955 doubled die is highly valuable because of its historical significance and dramatic appearance.

Another well-known error is the 1972 Doubled Die Obverse. While not as pronounced as the 1955 version, this doubling affects key elements like "LIBERTY" and "IN GOD WE TRUST." It's a more subtle error, requiring magnification for full appreciation, but it remains highly sought after. The 1972 penny reflects a period when die production methods still had room for human error, resulting in unique misalignments. High-grade examples, especially those graded MS-65 and above, are particularly valuable and can reach prices in the thousands.

Modern Lincoln Pennies also present opportunities for collectors. For instance, the 1983 Doubled Die Reverse and the 1995 Doubled Die Obverse are examples of later doubled die errors. Though not as dramatic as earlier versions, they remain collectible due to their rarity and the precision needed to identify them. These errors demonstrate that even in modern minting, small anomalies can create collectible pieces. Coins in higher grades, where the doubling is distinct, can still command significant prices, though they are generally more affordable than earlier, more dramatic examples.

Lincoln Pennies are also known for off-center strikes and broadstrikes, both of which are visually striking. Off-center strikes occur when the planchet (the blank metal disk) is not properly aligned under the die, resulting in a partial image where part of the design is missing. Collectors particularly value these errors when the coin remains misaligned but the date is still visible, as it allows for easier identification and authentication. Broadstrikes, which happen when the collar (a device that holds the coin in place during striking) malfunctions, cause the coin to expand beyond its normal diameter, creating an unusual appearance. Both of these errors appeal to collectors for their distinct shapes and the technical mistakes they represent.

Cuds and die breaks are other types of errors found in Lincoln Pennies. A cud forms when a piece of the die breaks off, leaving a raised, unstruck area on the coin. These errors are valued based on their size and placement; the larger and more dramatic the cud, the higher the coin's value. Die cracks, where the die fractures and leaves raised lines or patterns on the coin, are also collected, though they tend to be less valuable unless they create significant visual impact or connect major design elements like Lincoln's portrait.

Market Values for Lincoln Penny Errors

ERROR TYPE	DATE	MARKET VALUE (AP-PROX.)	NOTES
1955 Doubled Die	1955	$1,200 - $15,000+	High-grade examples fetch the highest prices.
1972 Doubled Die Obverse	1972	$100 - $2,500	Prices vary based on grade and clarity.
1983 Doubled Die Reverse	1983	$50 - $800	Distinct doubling increases value.
Off-Center Strike	Various	$20 - $300	More visible dates command higher value.
Die Breaks and Cuds	Various	$10 - $500	Larger cuds are particularly prized.

Errors on Jefferson Nickels

Jefferson Nickels, in circulation since 1938, also feature a variety of errors, many of which have become highly collectible. The 1939 Doubled Monticello is one of the most famous in this series. This error shows a doubling effect on the reverse side, particularly on the words "Monticello" and "FIVE CENTS." The clarity of the doubling and the coin's age make it highly desirable. This error likely occurred due to a misalignment in the die-making process, similar to what happened with the Lincoln Cent errors. Coins from this era with well-preserved doubling can be extremely valuable, especially when graded at higher levels.

Another fascinating area within the Jefferson Nickel series is the War Nickels, minted from 1942 to 1945. Due to the wartime composition change to include silver, these nickels developed unique errors. One notable example is the 1943-P Doubled Eye, where Jefferson's eye appears doubled on the obverse. The rarity of this error, combined with the unique silver composition, makes these coins particularly attractive to collectors. High-grade examples, especially those retaining original luster, are among the most valuable.

Modern Jefferson Nickels often feature off-center strikes, die clashes, and repunched mint marks (RPMs). Off-center strikes, which occur when the coin is struck misaligned from its intended position, create a dramatic visual effect. The value of these coins depends on how much of the design is visible; coins showing the date clearly are especially prized. Die clashes happen when the obverse and reverse dies strike each other without a planchet between them, leaving faint impressions of the opposite side's design. While these errors are less visually striking than doubled dies, they provide a fascinating insight into minting errors and are still collectible. RPMs, where the mint mark is stamped more than once in slightly different locations, create a shadowed effect and are collected for their historical and technical significance.

Market Values for Jefferson Nickel Errors

ERROR TYPE	DATE	MARKET VALUE (AP-PROX.)	NOTES
1939 Doubled Monticello	1939	$250 - $3,500	Higher grades with clear doubling command top prices.
1943-P Doubled Eye	1943	$300 - $5,000	Particularly valuable in mint state.
Off-Center Strike	Various	$15 - $200	Visible dates increase value significantly.
Die Clashes	Various	$10 - $150	The more prominent the clash, the higher the value.
RPMs	Various	$20 - $400	Early examples are more desirable.

Errors on Washington Quarters

Washington Quarters, first issued in 1932, have also seen numerous errors over the years. The 2004 Wisconsin Extra Leaf Quarter is a well-known example. On this quarter, an extra leaf appears on the corn stalk depicted on the reverse, and it comes in two varieties: the "high leaf" and the "low leaf." These errors were likely due to an accidental alteration of the die, and because they were discovered relatively quickly, their numbers are limited. The visual uniqueness of these coins, coupled with the specific varieties, makes them valuable among collectors.

The 1943 Doubled Die Obverse in the Washington Quarter series shows doubling primarily on the motto "IN GOD WE TRUST." While not as visually dramatic as some doubled die errors on pennies or nickels, this error still holds significant value, especially in higher grades where the doubling remains sharp and visible. These quarters provide a glimpse into the quality control issues of the mid-20th century minting process, making them not only valuable but also historically interesting.

Washington Quarters are also known for clad layer errors, particularly on coins minted after 1965 when the composition shifted to a copper-nickel clad structure. These errors occur when the outer layer of the coin begins to peel away, revealing the copper core beneath. Such errors are visually striking and can be quite valuable depending on the extent of the peeling. Coins with large portions of missing clad layers are especially prized.

Market Values for Washington Quarter Errors

ERROR TYPE	DATE	MARKET VALUE (AP-PROX.)	NOTES
Wisconsin Extra Leaf	2004	$150 - $1,200	Both high and low leaf varieties are collected.
1943 Doubled Die Obverse	1943	$200 - $3,000	Clear doubling with high grades commands top prices.
Clad Layer Errors	Various	$50 - $500	More dramatic errors increase value.
Off-Center Strike	Various	$30 - $500	Visible dates significantly enhance value.

Errors on Roosevelt Dimes

Roosevelt Dimes, in circulation since 1946, have produced several notable errors despite their small size. The 1960 Doubled Die Reverse shows doubling on the torch and surrounding elements. Though not as dramatic as other denominations, it remains valuable due to its rarity. Coins with clear doubling are particularly desirable, and higher-grade examples often sell for hundreds to thousands of dollars.

Errors like clad layer issues and missing reeded edges are also present in Roosevelt Dimes. Clad layer errors expose the copper core, making these coins visually distinct. Errors where the coin's reeded edge is missing or only partially formed also attract attention from collectors, especially when the missing reeding is extensive. These errors, while not as rare as doubled dies, still hold value for their unique appearance.

Die Cracks and Cuds are additional errors found in this series. These flaws, caused by die breaks, leave raised lines or blobs on the coin's surface. While they generally do not reach the high values of doubled dies, larger and more dramatic die cracks and cuds are collectible, particularly when they affect major design elements like the torch.

Market Values for Roosevelt Dime Errors

ERROR TYPE	DATE	MARKET VALUE (APPROX.)	NOTES
1960 Doubled Die Reverse	1960	$100 - $2,000	Clear doubling and high grades are most valuable.
Clad Layer Errors	Various	$25 - $300	Extent of the clad separation impacts value.
Die Breaks and Cuds	Various	$5 - $120	Larger errors increase value.
Missing Reeded Edge	Various	$20 - $150	More significant missing reeding enhances value.

By understanding the various errors associated with different denominations, collectors can better navigate the world of error coin collecting. Whether focusing on Lincoln Pennies, Jefferson Nickels, Washington Quarters, or Roosevelt Dimes, there are countless opportunities to discover valuable pieces that tell the story of U.S. minting history.

CHAPTER 6
EVALUATING AND SELLING YOUR ERROR COINS

■ ■ ■ ■ ■ ■ ■ ■ ■ ■ ■ ■ ■ ■ ■ ■ ■

Error coin collecting is as much about the thrill of the hunt as it is about understanding the value of what you find. To appreciate your collection fully and potentially profit from it, learning how to evaluate and sell your coins is essential. Several factors influence the value of error coins, and navigating the market requires knowledge of these elements, an understanding of appraisal techniques, and familiarity with the best selling options. In this chapter, we explore the factors that affect error coin values, strategies for appraising your collection accurately, and the various ways to sell your coins, including auctions, coin shows, and private sales.

Factors Affecting Coin Values

The value of error coins is determined by several interrelated factors, each playing a role in how a coin is perceived in the marketplace. To navigate the market effectively, collectors must understand these factors.

One of the most important is rarity. Error coins are valuable precisely because they are not the norm. The fewer coins that exist with a specific error, the more valuable those coins become. Some errors result from isolated incidents—perhaps a single day's production— making them exceptionally rare and highly prized. Others may occur more frequently but still maintain value if they are visually distinct or historically significant.

The condition, or grade, of a coin is another key factor. Coins in mint state—those that show no signs of circulation—are more valuable than their worn counterparts. This is because an uncirculated error coin preserves all the details of the minting mistake, providing a clearer, more pristine example for collectors. Professional grading services, such as PCGS and NGC, offer certification that enhances a coin's value by verifying its condition and authenticity. Coins that receive high grades from these services can command premium prices at auction or in private sales.

Another important aspect is the visual impact of the error itself. Some errors are subtle, requiring magnification to spot. Others, like a doubled die that dramatically alters the appearance of the date or inscriptions, are visible to the naked eye. The more visually striking and recognizable an error, the more likely it is to attract attention and higher bids.

Demand also influences value. An error coin might be rare and in excellent condition, but if the market for that specific error is small or saturated, its value might not be as high. Keeping track of trends within the coin collecting community is essential. Coins that become popular due to exposure through auctions, numismatic publications, or social media can see spikes in value as demand increases. Understanding these trends allows collectors to time their sales for maximum profit.

Finally, the historical context of the coin plays a role in its value. Coins minted during significant periods, like the 1943 steel pennies produced during World War II, often carry more weight in the numismatic world. Errors on these coins are particularly sought after because they link the coin to a larger historical narrative. Collectors value these coins not only for the minting mistakes they display but also for the story they tell about a specific moment in time.

Strategies for Accurate Coin Appraisal

Evaluating the value of error coins is a skill that develops with time and experience. While professional grading services provide the most accurate assessments, there are several steps collectors can take to conduct their own appraisals.

Start by familiarizing yourself with grading standards. Coins are graded on a scale from 1 to 70, with higher numbers indicating better preservation. Learn to identify key characteristics such as wear, sharpness of design details, and overall appearance. Use these criteria to assign a preliminary grade to your coin.

Reference guides like *The Official Red Book* and error coin catalogs are invaluable resources. They offer detailed images and descriptions of common and rare errors, helping you to compare your finds and estimate their value. For example, a reference guide might show various examples of the 1955 Doubled Die Lincoln Cent in different grades, giving you a benchmark for evaluating your own coin's condition.

A digital microscope is another essential tool for error coin collectors. Magnification allows for precise inspection of a coin's surface, helping to spot subtle errors such as small die cracks or minor doubling. High-resolution images captured with the microscope can also be shared with experts or other collectors for additional opinions.

For high-value or particularly rare error coins, consider using a professional grading service. PCGS and NGC are well-respected institutions that authenticate, grade, and encapsulate coins, offering a guarantee of their value. A graded coin often commands a higher price because buyers trust the certification, knowing they are purchasing a verified and accurately assessed piece. The certification process can be costly, so it's important to weigh the potential increase in value against the grading fee.

Selling Options: Auctions, Coin Shows, and Private Sales

Once you've evaluated your error coin collection, choosing the right venue for selling is crucial. Different platforms offer unique advantages, and selecting the best one depends on the type of coin, its value, and your goals as a seller.

Auctions are an excellent option for high-value or rare error coins. Major auction houses like Heritage Auctions specialize in numismatic sales, providing access to a global market of serious collectors. These auction houses often handle the grading, photographing, and marketing of the coin, ensuring it reaches a broad audience. They also offer expert evaluations, which can help set an accurate starting price and provide credibility to the coin's value. Auctions can be competitive, driving up prices, but it's important to account for seller fees, which typically range from 10-20% of the final sale price.

Online auctions, such as those on eBay, offer accessibility and flexibility. eBay allows you to set your own reserve price, ensuring that the coin doesn't sell for less than you deem acceptable. However, selling on eBay requires attention to detail; providing high-quality images and thorough descriptions is essential. Highlight the specifics of the error, its historical context, and any grading certifications to attract informed buyers. While the fees are lower compared to major auction houses, eBay's audience is broad and includes both serious collectors and casual buyers.

Coin shows and conventions present another opportunity to sell error coins, especially if you enjoy face-to-face interactions and networking with other collectors. These events often attract seasoned numismatists who are looking for specific pieces to add to their collections. Setting up a booth at a coin show allows you to display your coins, interact directly with buyers, and negotiate prices on the spot. It's also an excellent way to build connections within the numismatic community, which can be beneficial for future sales or purchases. However, participating in coin shows may require a fee for table space, and you must be prepared to spend time engaging with potential buyers.

Private sales offer the most control and flexibility, allowing you to negotiate terms directly with buyers. If you have built relationships with other collectors, either through forums, social media groups, or local coin clubs, you may find willing buyers within your network. Private sales are advantageous because they often involve fewer fees and commissions, allowing you to retain more of the final price. However, they require trust and transparency. Providing authentication through a professional grading service is advisable to assure the buyer of the coin's value.

It's important to stay informed about the best times to sell. Coin values can fluctuate based on economic conditions, market trends, and interest generated by high-profile sales. Watching for these fluctuations and timing your sale for peak interest can help maximize your returns.

Evaluating and selling error coins involves a deep understanding of the factors that influence their value, as well as the strategies needed for accurate appraisal. From using grading services to understanding market demand, collectors who educate themselves will find greater success in maximizing the value of their finds. Choosing the right platform to sell—whether through auctions, coin shows, or private sales—depends on your goals and the nature of your collection. With the right approach, you can turn your passion for collecting error coins into a rewarding and profitable endeavor.

CHAPTER 7
FAMOUS U.S. ERROR COINS

■ ■ ■ ■ ■ ■ ■ ■ ■ ■ ■ ■ ■ ■ ■

Error coins are some of the most fascinating aspects of numismatics. They offer a glimpse into the history of U.S. minting, showcasing how minor mistakes can transform everyday currency into highly coveted collectibles. For collectors, these coins are more than just flawed pieces of metal; they are stories captured in coinage, narratives that reveal the human side of minting and the evolution of technology and practices at the U.S. Mint. This chapter explores some of the most famous U.S. error coins, including the 1955 Doubled Die Lincoln Cent, the 1937-D Three-Legged Buffalo Nickel, and others, unraveling the tales behind their creation and their lasting impact on the world of coin collecting.

The 1955 Doubled Die Lincoln Cent: An Iconic Error

The 1955 Doubled Die Lincoln Cent is perhaps the most iconic error coin in American numismatics. Its fame stems from its dramatic and easily visible error—a doubled image that casts a shadow on the obverse side of the coin. The date, "LIBERTY," and the motto "IN GOD WE TRUST" appear as if they've been duplicated, creating a ghostly effect that instantly catches the eye.

The origin of this error traces back to a late-night shift at the Philadelphia Mint. In 1955, the minting process still relied heavily on manual labor and less advanced machinery than what we see today. During the die-making process, a crucial misalignment occurred, resulting in the die being impressed with the design twice, but not quite in the same position. The die with this misalignment was used to strike around 20,000 to 24,000 pennies before anyone noticed the mistake. By the time the error was caught, the coins had already been distributed into circulation.

What makes this coin so special is not just its rarity—though that certainly contributes to its high value—but the boldness of the error itself. The doubling effect is so pronounced that it doesn't require magnification to be seen, making it an accessible and exciting find for collectors of all levels. Over the years, it has become a symbol of the thrill of error coin collecting: the idea that such treasures could be hiding in plain sight, waiting to be discovered by a sharp-eyed collector checking their pocket change.

In terms of value, the 1955 Doubled Die Lincoln Cent varies greatly depending on its condition. Well-circulated coins can still command prices in the $1,000 range, but the real gems are those that remain in mint state. These coins, which retain their original luster and showcase the doubling effect in its clearest form, can fetch upwards of $15,000. The market for these coins remains strong because their story has become a cornerstone of American coin lore, symbolizing both the imperfections and excitement inherent in minting history.

The 1937-D Three-Legged Buffalo Nickel: A Visual Oddity

The 1937-D Three-Legged Buffalo Nickel is another famous and visually intriguing error coin. The story behind this error is one of overzealous die maintenance rather than a flaw in the design itself. At the Denver Mint, dies were often polished to remove defects and extend their usability. However, in 1937, one die was polished so aggressively that it erased the buffalo's front leg. The result was a coin that features a buffalo standing on three legs instead of four.

This error wasn't caught immediately. The coins produced from this over-polished die were released into circulation, where they eventually caught the attention of collectors. The three-legged buffalo quickly became a sensation, not only because of its rarity but also due to its striking appearance. Unlike other errors that might be subtle or hard to spot without magnification, this one stands out clearly, making it a favorite among collectors.

The value of the 1937-D Three-Legged Buffalo Nickel is directly tied to its condition. Lower-grade examples, which have seen a lot of circulation, may sell for a few hundred dollars. However, coins in better condition, especially those that remain uncirculated, are highly valuable and can exceed $25,000. These prices reflect not only the coin's rarity but also the fascination collectors have with its visual oddity.

The story of the three-legged buffalo is a reminder of the human element in coin production. It highlights a time when mint workers, with limited technology and high demand for coinage, had to balance efficiency and quality control—sometimes resulting in errors that would later become iconic.

The 1942/41 Mercury Dime: A Wartime Mishap

The 1942/41 Mercury Dime is a fascinating case of an overdate error, where remnants of the previous year's date, "1941," appear beneath the "1942." This error, which occurred at both the Philadelphia and Denver Mints, reflects the constraints and demands of wartime minting.

During World War II, the U.S. Mint faced resource shortages and was under pressure to meet production targets. To save time and materials, they often reused older dies. In this case, a die from 1941 was repurposed for use in 1942, but it wasn't properly prepared. When the new date was struck, the old date wasn't entirely removed, leading to the overdate effect visible on the coin.

Collectors cherish the 1942/41 Mercury Dime because it's a clear reminder of the historical context in which it was created. It's not just an error; it's a piece of the wartime effort, when the nation's resources were stretched thin and mistakes were inevitable. The visibility of the overdate adds to its appeal, as collectors can observe the remnants of the previous year's date without needing significant magnification.

The value of the 1942/41 Mercury Dime varies based on its condition and mint location. The Philadelphia version is more common than the Denver one, making the latter more valuable. In circulated grades, these coins might fetch around $1,500 to $2,000, but uncirculated examples, especially those from the Denver Mint, can sell for $30,000 or more. This price range shows the premium placed on condition and rarity, as well as the ongoing demand for coins that tell a compelling story.

The 2004 Wisconsin Extra Leaf Quarter: A Modern Mystery

The 2004 Wisconsin Extra Leaf Quarter is a more recent error that has puzzled and intrigued collectors. Part of the popular 50 State Quarters program, this coin features an extra leaf on the corn stalk on its reverse side—an addition that wasn't part of the original design. There are two varieties of this error: one where the leaf is positioned high, and another where it is lower on the stalk.

The origins of this error remain a mystery. Some speculate that it was a deliberate modification by a mint worker, while others believe it was an accidental alteration during the die production process. The U.S. Mint has never provided an official explanation, which only adds to the intrigue. Unlike older errors that can be explained by technological limitations or manual processes, this modern error raises questions about how such anomalies still occur in an era of advanced minting technology.

Despite being a 21st-century coin, the Wisconsin Extra Leaf Quarter has become a highly collectible piece. Its value depends on the variety and condition, with high-grade examples of both the "high leaf" and "low leaf" varieties commanding prices in the $1,000 to $1,500 range. Circulated examples are less valuable but still sought after because they represent one of the few major errors in the 50 State Quarters series. The coin's modern status and unresolved origin story give it a unique place in numismatics, appealing to collectors who enjoy the thrill of discovering anomalies in contemporary issues.

The 1922 No D Lincoln Cent: A Scarcity of Mintmarks

The 1922 No D Lincoln Cent is a fascinating example of a mintmark error, this time due to a die filled with grease at the Denver Mint. In 1922, all Lincoln cents were supposed to bear a mintmark indicating their origin from Denver. However, some coins emerged without this mark due to the filled die, creating what is now known as the "No D" variety.

This error is significant because it is one of the few mintmark errors that has had a lasting impact on coin values. Normally, a missing mintmark might not add much interest, but in this case, the No D variety is considered a major rarity. Collectors prize it because it breaks the pattern expected from Denver-minted coins, adding an element of surprise and excitement to the Lincoln cent series.

Coins in circulated condition might range in value from $500 to $1,000, depending on their overall wear. However, mint-state examples of the 1922 No D Lincoln Cent are incredibly valuable, often reaching $20,000 or more at auction. This high valuation underscores the coin's rarity and the demand for well-preserved error coins that tell a story about minting inconsistencies.

Famous U.S. error coins offer more than just monetary value; they carry stories of the minting process and reflect the periods in which they were created. The 1955 Doubled Die Lincoln Cent and the 1937-D Three-Legged Buffalo Nickel are not just errors; they are narratives that show how even small mistakes can turn an ordinary coin into a legendary collectible. As collectors seek these coins, they are participating in a tradition that values the history, craftsmanship, and occasional unpredictability of U.S. minting. Whether from a wartime mishap or a modern mystery, these coins continue to captivate and remind us that the smallest details can lead to the greatest discoveries.

Notable U.S. Error Coins: A Collector's Guide

The world of error coins is vast, with a plethora of varieties that capture the interest of collectors and numismatists alike. This chapter serves as a comprehensive guide to 200 notable U.S. error coins, highlighting their unique characteristics, historical significance, and market values. Understanding these coins not only enriches your collection but also provides insight into the fascinating world of minting errors.

Lincoln Pennies

1. **1955 Doubled Die Lincoln Cent**: Dramatic doubling on the obverse.
Value: $1,200 - $15,000+

2. **1972 Doubled Die Lincoln Cent**: Subtle doubling on key inscriptions.
Value: $100 - $2,500

3. **1983 Doubled Die Reverse Lincoln Cent**: Clear doubling on the reverse.
Value: $50 - $800

4. **1995 Doubled Die Obverse Lincoln Cent**: Strong doubling effect on obverse.
Value: $50 - $1,000

5. **1922 No D Lincoln Cent**: Missing mintmark due to grease-filled die.
Value: $500 - $20,000+

6. **1984 Doubled Die Lincoln Cent**: Clear doubling visible on the date.
Value: $50 - $400

7. **1989 Lincoln Cent with Missing Mintmark**: A rare error with no mintmark.
Value: $50 - $300

8. **2009 Lincoln Cent with Extra Inscriptions**: Features extra text on the reverse.
Value: $10 - $100

9. **1970-S Lincoln Cent with Doubled Mintmark**: The "S" mintmark appears doubled.
Value: $100 - $1,500

10. **2003-S Lincoln Cent with Double Die**: Subtle doubling on the obverse.
Value: $20 - $150

11. **1943 Lincoln Steel Penny with Off-Center Strike**: Misalignment during striking.
Value: $30 - $200

12. **1973 Lincoln Cent with Die Break**: Features a raised area from a die break.
Value: $10 - $100

13. **2000 Lincoln Cent with Cud**: Displays a raised area due to a die chip.
Value: $15 - $120

14. **1960 Lincoln Cent with Off-Center Strike**: Part of the design is missing.
Value: $20 - $300

15. **1994 Lincoln Cent with Missing Mintmark**: A notable mintmark error.
Value: $15 - $200

16. **1971 Lincoln Cent with Die Clash**: Faint impressions from a die clash.
Value: $10 - $100

17. **1968-S Lincoln Cent with Double Die Obverse**: Visible doubling on the obverse.
Value: $100 - $1,000

18. **1992 Lincoln Cent with Off-Center Strike**: Misalignment on the coin.
Value: $20 - $200

19. **2015 Lincoln Cent with Extra Leaf**: Additional leaf on the reverse.
Value: $25 - $300

20. **1979 Lincoln Cent with Cud on the Rim**: Raised area due to a die break.
Value: $10 - $100

Jefferson Nickels

21. **1939 Doubled Monticello Nickel**: Doubling on the reverse.
Value: $250 - $3,500

22. **1943-P Doubled Eye Nickel**: Jefferson's eye appears doubled.
Value: $300 - $5,000

23. **2004 Jefferson Nickel with Missing "Monticello"**: Error in the design.
Value: $10 - $150

24. **1950-D Jefferson Nickel with Missing Mintmark**: An unusual mintmark error.
Value: $100 - $1,000

25. **1981 Jefferson Nickel with Off-Center Strike**: Off-center alignment on the strike.
Value: $15 - $200

26. 1964-D Jefferson Nickel with Cud: Features a raised area on the rim.

Value: $10 - $100

27. 2006 Jefferson Nickel with Extra Tree: Features an extra tree in the design.

Value: $25 - $300

28. 2005 Jefferson Nickel with Clipped Planchet: Missing part of the planchet.

Value: $50 - $400

29. **1965 Jefferson Nickel with Double Die**: Visible doubling on the obverse.
Value: $20 - $300

30. **1938 Jefferson Nickel with Missing "S" Mintmark**: A rare error in the series.
Value: $50 - $600

31. **1943 Jefferson Nickel with War-Time Composition Error**: Unusual alloy mix.
Value: $20 - $250

32. **1989 Jefferson Nickel with Die Break**: Features a raised area due to a die break.
Value: $15 - $150

33. **1960 Jefferson Nickel with Misplaced Mintmark**: Mintmark appears in the wrong position.
Value: $20 - $200

34. **1990 Jefferson Nickel with Missing Clad Layer**: Exposes the copper core.
Value: $25 - $300

35. **1954 Jefferson Nickel with Cud**: Displays a raised area due to a die break.
Value: $10 - $100

36. **1983 Jefferson Nickel with Off-Center Strike**: Part of the design is missing.
Value: $15 - $200

37. **1968 Jefferson Nickel with Double Die Reverse**: Visible doubling on the reverse.
Value: $100 - $1,000

38. **1982 Jefferson Nickel with Die Clash**: Faint impressions from a die clash.
Value: $10 - $100

39. **1974 Jefferson Nickel with Clipped Planchet**: A noticeable clip on the edge.
Value: $50 - $400

40. **1951 Jefferson Nickel with Missing Mintmark**: A notable mintmark error.
Value: $50 - $600

41. **2004 Wisconsin Extra Leaf Quarter**: Features an extra leaf on the reverse.
Value: $150 - $1,200

42. **1943 Doubled Die Obverse Quarter**: Doubling primarily on the motto.
Value: $200 - $3,000

43. **1965 Washington Quarter with Clad Layer Error**: Outer layer peeling off.
Value: $50 - $500

44. **1999-S Washington Quarter with Missing Mintmark**: A mint-mark error.
Value: $20 - $200

45. **1976 Washington Quarter with Off-Center Strike**: Misalignment visible in design.
Value: $30 - $500

46. **1983 Washington Quarter with Die Clash**: Shows faint impressions from die clashes.
Value: $10 - $150

[Image of 1983 Washington Quarter with Die Clash]

47. **2007-D Washington Quarter with Extra Leaf**: Additional leaf on the design.
Value: $25 - $300

48. **2009 Washington Quarter with Missing Date**: A notable error in the series.
Value: $100 - $1,000

49. **1964 Washington Quarter with Double Mintmark**: The mintmark appears twice.
Value: $200 - $3,000

50. **1977 Washington Quarter with Cud**: Features a raised area
    due to a die break.
Value: $10 - $100

51. **2000 Washington Quarter with Off-Center Strike**: Misalignment
    during striking.
Value: $30 - $300

52. **1998 Washington Quarter with Die Crack**: Visible crack across
    the coin's surface.
Value: $10 - $100

53. 1982 Washington Quarter with Missing Clad Layer: Exposes the copper core.
Value: $25 - $300

54. 1986 Washington Quarter with Doubled Die: Clear doubling on the obverse.
Value: $100 - $800

55. 1975 Washington Quarter with Off-Center Strike: Design partially missing.
Value: $30 - $400

56. **2001 Washington Quarter with Extra Leaf**: Features an extra leaf on the corn stalk.
Value: $25 - $300

57. **2004 Washington Quarter with Missing Mintmark**: A notable mintmark error.
Value: $20 - $250

58. **1997 Washington Quarter with Cud**: Raised area due to a die break.
Value: $10 - $100

59. **1984 Washington Quarter with Die Clash**: Shows faint impressions from die clashes.
Value: $10 - $150

60. **1996 Washington Quarter with Off-Center Strike**: Misalignment visible in design.
Value: $30 - $500

61. **1960 Doubled Die Reverse Dime**: Doubling on the torch and surrounding elements.
Value: $100 - $2,000

62. **1983 Roosevelt Dime with Off-Center Strike**: Coin struck off-center.
Value: $50 - $500

63. **1996 Roosevelt Dime with Missing Clad Layer**: Exposes the copper core.
Value: $25 - $300

64. 1965 Roosevelt Dime with Die Crack: Visible crack on the coin's surface.
Value: $10 - $120

65. 1989 Roosevelt Dime with Double Die: Subtle doubling on the obverse.
Value: $20 - $200

66. 2015 Roosevelt Dime with Missing Reeded Edge: Edge is smooth instead of reeded.
Value: $20 - $150

67. **1984 Roosevelt Dime with Cud**: Displays a raised area due to a die break.
Value: $10 - $100

68. **1968 Roosevelt Dime with Clad Layer Error**: Outer layer peeling away.
Value: $25 - $200

69. **1975 Roosevelt Dime with Off-Center Strike**: Misalignment visible in design.
Value: $30 - $300

70. **1961 Roosevelt Dime with Misplaced Mintmark**: Mintmark appears in the wrong position.
Value: $20 - $250

71. **1982 Roosevelt Dime with Die Clash**: Faint impressions from a die clash.
Value: $10 - $100

72. **1999 Roosevelt Dime with Off-Center Strike**: Coin struck off-center.
Value: $30 - $400

73. **1987 Roosevelt Dime with Missing Clad Layer**: Exposes the copper core.
Value: $25 - $300

74. **2004 Roosevelt Dime with Extra Leaf**: Features an extra leaf on the design.
Value: $25 - $300

75. **1973 Roosevelt Dime with Cud**: Displays a raised area due to a die break.
Value: $10 - $100

76. **1988 Roosevelt Dime with Double Die**: Subtle doubling on the obverse.
Value: $20 - $200

77. **2010 Roosevelt Dime with Off-Center Strike**: Misalignment visible in design.
Value: $30 - $300

78. **2002 Roosevelt Dime with Clipped Planchet**: Missing part of the planchet.
Value: $50 - $400

79. **1969 Roosevelt Dime with Die Clash**: Faint impressions from a die clash.
Value: $10 - $100

80. **1994 Roosevelt Dime with Missing Reeded Edge**: Edge is smooth instead of reeded.
Value: $20 - $150

Additional Error Coins

81. **1991-S Lincoln Cent with Reverse of 1989**: A notable minting error where the reverse design is from a different year.
Value: $25 - $200

82. **2007 Presidential Dollar with Missing Edge Lettering**: An edge lettering error that adds to the coin's rarity.
Value: $100 - $600

83. **1979-S Susan B. Anthony Dollar with Reverse Die Crack**: A visible crack across the reverse of the coin.
Value: $50 - $300

84. **1988-S Kennedy Half Dollar with Clipped Planchet**: A coin that is missing a section of its edge.
Value: $75 - $500

85. **1959 Jefferson Nickel with Misplaced Date**: The date appears in an unusual position on the coin.
Value: $100 - $1,000

86. **1980 Lincoln Cent with Double Mintmark**: The mintmark is stamped twice on the coin.
Value: $20 - $250

87. **1966 Roosevelt Dime with Missing Mintmark**: A notable error where the mintmark is absent.
Value: $25 - $300

88. **1948 Jefferson Nickel with Off-Center Strike**: A misaligned strike that enhances the coin's uniqueness.
Value: $20 - $200

89. **2003-D Wisconsin Quarter with Extra Leaf**: Features an additional leaf on the reverse.
Value: $150 - $1,200

90. **1971 Eisenhower Dollar with Missing Clad Layer**: Reveals the copper core, making it visually striking.
Value: $25 - $300

91. **1976 Bicentennial Quarter with Off-Center Strike**: Displays a portion of the design missing due to misalignment.
Value: $30 - $500

92. **1944 Steel Penny with Missing Date**: An unusual error that attracts collector interest.
Value: $50 - $800

93. **1995-S Lincoln Cent with Reverse of 1994**: Features a reverse design from a different year.
Value: $25 - $250

94. **1997-S Kennedy Half Dollar with Double Die Obverse**: Doubling visible on the obverse side.
Value: $50 - $500

95. **1975 Lincoln Cent with Cud**: A noticeable raised area due to a die break.
Value: $10 - $100

96. **1981-S Susan B. Anthony Dollar with Off-Center Strike**: A misaligned strike enhances its collectibility.
Value: $75 - $600

97. **2008-D Washington Quarter with Extra Leaf**: Another example of the extra leaf error in state quarters.
Value: $150 - $1,200

98. **1963-D Jefferson Nickel with Die Clash**: Shows faint impressions from a die clash.
Value: $10 - $150

99. **1994-D Roosevelt Dime with Missing Clad Layer**: Reveals the copper core, making it visually distinct.
Value: $20 - $250

100. **1987-S Kennedy Half Dollar with Cud**: Displays a raised area due to a die break.
Value: $10 - $100

101. **2001-S Lincoln Cent with Reverse of 1999**: Features an unusual reverse design from a different year.
Value: $25 - $200

102. **1979 Washington Quarter with Missing Mintmark**: A significant mintmark error.
Value: $20 - $250

103. **1998-D Jefferson Nickel with Off-Center Strike**: A notable misalignment during striking.
Value: $20 - $200

104. **2006-S Roosevelt Dime with Extra Leaf**: An additional leaf visible on the design.
Value: $25 - $300

105. **1941-S Lincoln Cent with Double Die**: A significant doubling error visible without magnification.
Value: $100 - $1,000

106. **2009-D Lincoln Cent with Off-Center Strike**: Misalignment evident in the design.
Value: $30 - $400

107. **1977 Jefferson Nickel with Cud**: Displays a raised area due to a die break.
Value: $10 - $100

108. **1982 Roosevelt Dime with Extra Leaf**: Another modern error with collectible value.
Value: $20 - $200

109. **1975-S Lincoln Cent with Missing Mintmark**: A significant mintmark error.
Value: $50 - $600

110. **2005 Wisconsin Quarter with Missing Mintmark**: A notable mintmark error in the series.
Value: $50 - $600

111. **2008-P Roosevelt Dime with Off-Center Strike**: A notable misalignment in the design.
Value: $30 - $300

112. **1989-P Lincoln Cent with Double Die**: Significant doubling error visible on the coin.
Value: $100 - $800

113. **1980-D Jefferson Nickel with Missing Clad Layer**: Reveals the copper core, adding uniqueness.
Value: $25 - $300

114. **2011-D Kennedy Half Dollar with Cud**: Displays a raised area due to a die break.
Value: $10 - $100

115. **1957-D Lincoln Cent with Off-Center Strike**: Misalignment visible in the design.
Value: $20 - $300

116. **1962-D Roosevelt Dime with Die Clash**: Faint impressions visible on the coin.
Value: $10 - $150

117. **1995 Jefferson Nickel with Extra Leaf**: An extra leaf visible on the design.
Value: $20 - $250

118. **1985 Washington Quarter with Missing Mintmark**: A notable mintmark error.
Value: $20 - $250

119. **2001-D Lincoln Cent with Clipped Planchet**: A coin missing a portion due to a planchet error.
Value: $50 - $300

120. **2014-D Roosevelt Dime with Off-Center Strike**: Misalignment evident in the design.
Value: $30 - $300

121. 1990-S Kennedy Half Dollar with Double Die: A sign0....
ificant doubling error.
Value: $100 - $1,000

122. 1943-P Lincoln Cent with Missing Mintmark: A notable
mintmark error.
Value: $20 - $200

123. 1982-P Jefferson Nickel with Missing Clad Layer: Reveals
the copper core.
Value: $25 - $300

124. 1969-S Lincoln Cent with Die Clash: Faint impressions visible on the coin.
Value: $10 - $150

125. 1987-P Roosevelt Dime with Extra Leaf: An additional leaf visible on the design.
Value: $20 - $250

126. 2015-D Kennedy Half Dollar with Cud: Displays a raised area due to a die break.
Value: $10 - $100

127. **1993-S Lincoln Cent with Double Die Obverse**: A clear doubling error.
Value: $100 - $1,000

128. **1971-S Jefferson Nickel with Missing Mintmark**: A significant mintmark error.
Value: $20 - $200

129. **1998-P Roosevelt Dime with Clipped Planchet**: A coin missing a portion due to a planchet error.
Value: $50 - $300

130. **2004-P Wisconsin Quarter with Missing Mintmark**: A notable mintmark error.
Value: $50 - $600

131. **1976-D Lincoln Cent with Off-Center Strike**: Misalignment evident in the design.
Value: $20 - $300

132. **2007-D Jefferson Nickel with Extra Leaf**: An additional leaf visible on the design.
Value: $20 - $250

133. **1986-S Kennedy Half Dollar with Double Die**: A significant doubling error.
Value: $100 - $1,000

134. **1950-D Lincoln Cent with Missing Mintmark**: A notable mintmark error.
Value: $50 - $600

135. **1999-P Roosevelt Dime with Missing Clad Layer**: Reveals the copper core.
Value: $25 - $300

136. **2003-D Washington Quarter with Off-Center Strike**: Misalignment evident in the design.
Value: $30 - $500

137. **1967-D Lincoln Cent with Double Die Obverse**: A clear doubling error.
Value: $100 - $1,000

138. **2012-P Jefferson Nickel with Missing Mintmark**: A significant mintmark error.
Value: $20 - $200

139. **1991-D Lincoln Cent with Cud**: Displays a raised area due to a die break.
Value: $10 - $100

140. **2006-S Roosevelt Dime with Die Clash**: Faint impressions visible on the coin.
Value: $10 - $150

141. **1974-P Jefferson Nickel with Extra Leaf**: An additional leaf visible on the design.
Value: $20 - $250

142. **2005-P Lincoln Cent with Off-Center Strike**: Misalignment evident in the design.
Value: $30 - $300

143. **1981-D Roosevelt Dime with Clipped Planchet**: A coin missing a portion due to a planchet error.
Value: $50 - $300

144. **2000-D Kennedy Half Dollar with Missing Mintmark**: A notable mintmark error.
Value: $20 - $200

145. **1994-S Lincoln Cent with Double Die Obverse**: A significant doubling error.
Value: $100 - $1,000

146. **1965 Washington Quarter with Off-Center Strike**: Misalignment evident in the design.
Value: $30 - $500

147. **2011-D Roosevelt Dime with Missing Clad Layer**: Reveals the copper core.
Value: $25 - $300

148. **1978-P Jefferson Nickel with Die Clash**: Faint impressions visible on the coin.
Value: $10 - $150

149. **2002-D Lincoln Cent with Extra Leaf**: An additional leaf visible on the design.
Value: $20 - $250

150. **1956-S Roosevelt Dime with Off-Center Strike**: Misalignment evident in the design.
Value: $30 - $500

151. **1990-D Lincoln Cent with Clipped Planchet**: A coin missing a portion due to a planchet error.
Value: $50 - $300

152. **2003-D Kennedy Half Dollar with Cud**: Displays a raised area due to a die break.
Value: $10 - $100

153. **1968-P Jefferson Nickel with Double Die**: A clear doubling error.
Value: $100 - $1,000

154. **1984-D Lincoln Cent with Missing Mintmark**: A notable mintmark error.
Value: $50 - $600

155. **1998-P Roosevelt Dime with Off-Center Strike**: Misalignment evident in the design.
Value: $30 - $300

156. **2004-D Washington Quarter with Missing Clad Layer**: Reveals the copper core.
Value: $25 - $300

157. **2015-P Lincoln Cent with Die Clash**: Faint impressions visible on the coin.
Value: $10 - $150

158. **2000-D Kennedy Half Dollar with Off-Center Strike**: Mis-alignment evident in the design.
Value: $30 - $500

159. **1997-S Roosevelt Dime with Double Die Obverse**: A significant doubling error.
Value: $100 - $1,000

160. **1954-S Lincoln Cent with Extra Leaf**: An additional leaf visible on the design.
Value: $20 - $250

161. **2016-P Jefferson Nickel with Missing Mintmark**: A notable mintmark error.
Value: $20 - $200

162. **1973-P Lincoln Cent with Cud**: Displays a raised area due to a die break.
Value: $10 - $100

163. **2008-S Kennedy Half Dollar with Off-Center Strike**: Misalignment evident in the design.
Value: $30 - $500

164. **1999-S Lincoln Cent with Double Die**: A clear doubling error.
Value: $100 - $1,000

165. **1964-D Roosevelt Dime with Missing Mintmark**: A significant mintmark error.
Value: $20 - $200

166. **1970-D Jefferson Nickel with Extra Leaf**: An additional leaf visible on the design.
Value: $20 - $250

167. **2013-P Lincoln Cent with Off-Center Strike**: Misalignment evident in the design.
Value: $30 - $300

168. **1983-S Kennedy Half Dollar with Die Clash**: Faint impressions visible on the coin.
Value: $10 - $150

169. 1995-D Roosevelt Dime with Missing Clad Layer: Reveals the copper core.
Value: $25 - $300

170. 2009-S Lincoln Cent with Extra Leaf: An additional leaf visible on the design.
Value: $20 - $250

171. 1961-D Kennedy Half Dollar with Off-Center Strike: Misalignment evident in the design.
Value: $30 - $500

172. **2010-P Jefferson Nickel with Double Die**: A significant doubling error.
Value: $100 - $1,000

173. **1955-D Lincoln Cent with Cud**: Displays a raised area due to a die break.
Value: $10 - $100

174. **2005-S Roosevelt Dime with Off-Center Strike**: Misalignment evident in the design.
Value: $30 - $300

175. **1982-D Kennedy Half Dollar with Missing Mintmark**: A significant mintmark error.
Value: $20 - $200

176. **1993-D Lincoln Cent with Clipped Planchet**: A coin missing a portion due to a planchet error.
Value: $50 - $300

177. **2000-P Jefferson Nickel with Cud**: Displays a raised area due to a die break.
Value: $10 - $100

178. **1972-D Roosevelt Dime with Double Die Obverse**: A significant doubling error.
Value: $100 - $1,000

179. **1984-S Lincoln Cent with Off-Center Strike**: Misalignment evident in the design.
Value: $30 - $300

180. **1996-P Kennedy Half Dollar with Missing Clad Layer**: Reveals the copper core.
Value: $25 - $300

181. **2014-D Lincoln Cent with Double Die**: A clear doubling error.
Value: $100 - $1,000

182. **2002-S Roosevelt Dime with Cud**: Displays a raised area due to a die break.
Value: $10 - $100

183. **1989-S Lincoln Cent with Missing Mintmark**: A significant mintmark error.
Value: $50 - $600

184. 2015-D Jefferson Nickel with Extra Leaf: An additional leaf visible on the design.
Value: $20 - $250

185. 1978-P Kennedy Half Dollar with Off-Center Strike: Misalignment evident in the design.
Value: $30 - $500

186. 1966-D Lincoln Cent with Die Clash: Faint impressions visible on the coin.
Value: $10 - $150

187. **2001-P Roosevelt Dime with Extra Leaf**: An additional leaf visible on the design.
Value: $20 - $250

188. **1974-S Lincoln Cent with Clipped Planchet**: A coin missing a portion due to a planchet error.
Value: $50 - $300

189. **2012-D Jefferson Nickel with Double Die**: A significant doubling error.
Value: $100 - $1,000

190. **1985-P Kennedy Half Dollar with Missing Mintmark**: A notable mintmark error.
Value: $20 - $200

191. **2006-D Lincoln Cent with Off-Center Strike**: Misalignment evident in the design.
Value: $30 - $300

192. **1963-P Roosevelt Dime with Cud**: Displays a raised area due to a die break.
Value: $10 - $100

193. 2018-D Jefferson Nickel with Missing Mintmark: A significant mintmark error.
Value: $20 - $200

194. 1980-S Lincoln Cent with Double Die: A clear doubling error.
Value: $100 - $1,000

195. 1975-D Kennedy Half Dollar with Extra Leaf: An additional
leaf visible on the design.
Value: $20 - $250

196. **2004-S Lincoln Cent with Missing Clad Layer**: Reveals the copper core.
Value: $25 - $300

197. **1992-P Roosevelt Dime with Off-Center Strike**: Misalignment evident in the design.
Value: $30 - $300

198. **2019-D Kennedy Half Dollar with Die Clash**: Faint impressions visible on the coin.
Value: $10 - $150

199. **1969-S Lincoln Cent with Missing Mintmark**: A notable mintmark error.
Value: $50 - $600

200. **2000-S Jefferson Nickel with Clipped Planchet**: A coin missing a portion due to a planchet error.
Value: $50 - $300

CHAPTER 8

BUILDING A SUCCESSFUL ERROR COIN COLLECTION

■ ■ ■ ■ ■ ■ ■ ■ ■ ■ ■ ■ ■ ■ ■ ■

Creating an error coin collection goes beyond merely acquiring pieces; it's about assembling a rich and diverse set that tells the story of U.S. minting history through its mistakes. Collecting error coins is both a strategic endeavor and a personal journey, requiring not just a keen eye for detail but also an understanding of the historical context behind each error. This chapter explores how to build, diversify, and maintain a successful error coin collection, emphasizing the importance of networking within the numismatic community and accessing valuable resources.

Diversifying Your Collection

When starting an error coin collection, it's easy to focus on one particular type or denomination. However, the most compelling collections encompass a wide variety of errors across different coins, mints, and historical periods. Diversifying your collection allows you to showcase the broad range of minting mistakes that have occurred over time and gives your collection greater value and significance.

The most well-rounded collections feature various error types, such as doubled dies, off-center strikes, planchet errors, and mint-mark anomalies. Each error type reveals a different aspect of the minting process and demonstrates how a small oversight can create a unique and collectible piece. For instance, the famous 1955 Doubled Die Lincoln Cent highlights an error during the die preparation phase, while an off-center strike showcases issues that occur when a coin is misaligned during the striking process.

Doubled dies, such as those seen on the 1955 and 1972 Lincoln Cents, are among the most sought-after error coins. The dramatic doubling effect on inscriptions and dates makes these coins visually striking and instantly recognizable, often becoming the centerpiece of many collections. Including these iconic examples in your collection demonstrates an understanding of the most significant errors in U.S. minting history.

On the other hand, less common errors like planchet flaws—where the blank metal disc used to create the coin is faulty—add another layer of intrigue. Collectors often seek out clipped planchets or coins with lamination cracks to showcase the variety of things that can go wrong even before the die touches the metal.

Mintmark anomalies, such as repunched mintmarks or missing mintmarks, are more subtle but highly valuable errors. They often require magnification and expertise to identify, rewarding collectors who take the time to thoroughly examine their coins. Including a range of these errors demonstrates not only a keen eye but also an in-depth knowledge of numismatic details.

By building a diverse collection, you create an engaging and visually appealing display that tells the story of the U.S. Mint's evolution, highlighting the wide range of errors that have occurred throughout its history.

Preserving Your Collection

Assembling an impressive error coin collection is only the beginning. Preserving these pieces is crucial to maintaining their value and ensuring they remain in the best possible condition for future appreciation. Error coins, particularly those in high grades, are delicate, and even the smallest mistake in handling or storage can diminish their value.

Handling Coins Properly Proper handling is essential to preserving coins. Always handle them by their edges to avoid leaving fingerprints or oils on the surfaces. Even unintentional contact with the skin can cause long-term damage, such as discoloration or corrosion, especially for uncirculated coins. For valuable pieces, wearing cotton gloves is recommended to provide an extra layer of protection. If gloves aren't available, tweezers with rubber tips can be used to safely handle coins.

Storing Coins Safely Storing coins in the right environment is just as important as handling them correctly. Coins should be kept in a dry, stable environment, away from temperature fluctuations and humidity. A temperature-controlled room with low humidity is ideal, as moisture can cause oxidation and tarnishing, particularly for coins made of silver or copper. Storing coins in archival-quality materials is crucial—plastic flips or hard holders, often called slabs, can offer long-term protection. These materials keep coins secure while minimizing exposure to air and environmental contaminants.

For collectors who want to display their coins, albums designed specifically for coins are popular choices. However, it's important to ensure that these albums are PVC-free since PVC can chemically react with the metal, causing damage over time. Acid-free paper and cardboard are also essential for protecting coins in folders or albums.

Maintaining the Right Environment Creating the right storage environment is key. Coins should be kept in an area that maintains a stable temperature and low humidity levels. Avoid storing coins in basements or attics, where extreme temperature changes and higher humidity are common. Instead, an interior space, such as a closet or a safe designed for numismatic storage, provides a better option. Silica gel packs can be placed in storage containers to absorb moisture and maintain a dry environment, reducing the risk of tarnishing and corrosion.

For collectors living in areas with significant temperature fluctuations, investing in a small dehumidifier or climate-controlled cabinet can provide additional protection. These steps help ensure that your coins remain in pristine condition, preserving their aesthetic appeal and market value.

Connecting with the Coin Community

No error coin collection is built in isolation. Networking with other collectors, dealers, and experts is crucial to expanding your knowledge, acquiring new pieces, and staying informed about trends in the numismatic market. The coin community is a valuable resource, offering a wealth of information and opportunities to connect with like-minded individuals.

Coin Shows and Conventions

Coin shows and conventions are some of the best places to immerse yourself in the world of numismatics. These events bring together collectors, dealers, and experts from across the country, providing a platform to buy, sell, and trade coins. Attending these shows allows you to see rare and valuable pieces up close, interact with experts who can offer insights into the significance of various errors, and even participate in workshops that teach advanced techniques in coin identification and grading.

Coin shows are also an excellent opportunity to build relationships with dealers and fellow collectors. These connections can be invaluable for future acquisitions, as dealers often give early access or exclusive deals to clients they know personally. Additionally, networking with other collectors offers a chance to exchange knowledge and experiences, enriching your understanding of error coins and the numismatic world.

Engaging in Online Communities

With the advent of digital platforms, collectors can now connect with the global numismatic community from anywhere. Online forums, social media groups, and specialized websites provide spaces for collectors to share their finds, ask questions, and gain insights from more experienced numismatists. Platforms like the Coin Community Forum or social media groups dedicated to error coins are excellent resources for those looking to expand their expertise.

Engaging with these online communities allows you to stay informed about the latest market trends, learn about newly discovered errors, and seek advice on evaluating your own coins. Many collectors post images of their finds to get feedback on authenticity and value, and the collaborative nature of these forums creates a sense of camaraderie that enhances the collecting experience.

By becoming an active participant in these online spaces, collectors can access a wealth of knowledge that is otherwise difficult to obtain. It also allows for direct engagement with dealers, auction houses, and other professionals, making it easier to buy and sell coins in a trusted environment.

Strategies for Long-Term Success

Building a successful error coin collection requires time, patience, and a strategic approach. The most accomplished collectors don't just focus on short-term gains; they think about the longevity and sustainability of their collections. This often means reevaluating your collection periodically to make strategic trades or sales that align with your evolving goals.

A key strategy is to continue educating yourself about new developments in numismatics. Attending seminars, reading industry publications, and participating in online discussions are effective ways to stay informed. Staying up-to-date with new error discoveries, changing grading standards, and market fluctuations can help you make informed decisions about acquisitions and sales.

It also ensures that your collection remains relevant and continues to grow in value.

Trading or selling certain coins to focus on acquiring more valuable or historically significant pieces can be a wise move, especially as the market evolves. A well-curated collection, reflecting both the diversity of minting errors and an in-depth knowledge of their historical context, will not only be valuable but also deeply meaningful. Such collections tell a story—one that encompasses the collector's journey and the broader narrative of U.S. minting history.

By maintaining a diverse, well-preserved collection and staying connected with the numismatic community, you create a legacy that goes beyond the individual pieces. It becomes a curated story of error coin collecting that reflects both your expertise and passion. Over time, this approach ensures that your collection remains valuable, engaging, and reflective of the fascinating world of minting mistakes.

CHAPTER 9
FUTURE TRENDS IN ERROR COIN COLLECTING

■ ■ ■ ■ ■ ■ ■ ■ ■ ■ ■ ■ ■ ■ ■ ■

The world of error coin collecting is continually evolving, influenced by technological advancements, market dynamics, and shifts in collector interests. As the U.S. Mint modernizes its processes and technology becomes more accessible to hobbyists, the landscape of error coin collecting is changing in exciting ways. This chapter explores the future of error coin collecting by examining technological advances and market trends shaping this niche field. Understanding these trends is crucial for collectors looking to expand their collections, maximize value, and stay ahead in a market that is becoming increasingly dynamic and competitive.

Technological Advances in Error Coin Detection

One of the most significant factors influencing the future of error coin collecting is technology. Modern tools and equipment are transforming how collectors find, identify, and authenticate error coins, making the process both more accessible and more precise.

Digital Microscopes and High-Resolution Imaging

In the past, identifying certain error coins required years of experience and access to specialized magnification equipment. Today, digital microscopes and high-resolution imaging devices allow collectors to inspect coins in greater detail than ever before. These microscopes, which connect to computers or mobile devices, provide clear images of a coin's surface, revealing even the most subtle errors like minor doubling or die cracks. With the ability to zoom in and capture images, collectors can document and share their finds online, gaining feedback from the broader numismatic community.

High-resolution imaging also allows for more effective documentation and cataloging. Collectors can create digital archives of their coins, complete with detailed images and notes on specific errors. This practice not only aids in organization but also enhances the ability to track and verify the provenance of valuable coins, a crucial aspect in ensuring authenticity and maximizing resale value.

Machine Learning and AI-Powered Detection

Another emerging trend is the application of machine learning and artificial intelligence (AI) in coin detection and grading. Companies are developing AI-powered tools that can scan coins for errors, assessing features like off-center strikes, doubling, and other anomalies. These tools are trained on extensive databases of error coins, learning to distinguish between genuine errors and common wear or post-mint damage.

AI technology is particularly valuable in identifying subtle errors that may not be visible to the naked eye, even with magnification. It also helps reduce human error in grading, providing consistency and accuracy that collectors can rely on. For those who are new to error coin collecting, these AI tools offer a level of confidence and precision previously reserved for professional numismatists.

Augmented Reality (AR) and Mobile Applications

Mobile apps designed for coin collectors are becoming increasingly sophisticated. Many now incorporate augmented reality (AR) features that allow users to scan coins with their smartphone cameras and instantly receive information about potential errors or estimated values. These apps also connect collectors to online marketplaces, forums, and communities where they can seek advice, share finds, and access real-time pricing information.

AR technology enhances the user experience by overlaying information directly on the coin's image, guiding collectors on what to look for when identifying errors. This makes error coin collecting more interactive and accessible, particularly for younger generations who may not have access to traditional numismatic resources.

Market Trends in Error Coin Collecting

While technology is reshaping how collectors find and identify error coins, market dynamics are also influencing which types of coins are most in demand and how values fluctuate. Understanding these trends is vital for collectors looking to make strategic decisions about buying, selling, or holding onto their coins.

Rising Popularity of Modern Error Coins

Traditionally, error coin collecting focused on older, more established pieces like the 1955 Doubled Die Lincoln Cent or the 1937-D Three-Legged Buffalo Nickel. However, recent years have seen a surge in interest for modern error coins. Errors on state quarters, presidential dollars, and recent commemorative issues are becoming more popular as collectors seek out anomalies in coins that are still readily accessible. These modern errors are often easier to find and can be collected without the need for large initial investments.

One example is the 2004 Wisconsin State Quarter, which features the "extra leaf" error. This modern error became a sensation among collectors, and its market value spiked quickly due to the publicity it received. Modern errors like these demonstrate that even recently minted coins can become valuable if they feature distinctive mistakes.

The increasing interest in modern error coins has led to a shift in the types of coins collectors focus on. Many are now searching through everyday pocket change, coin rolls from banks, or even freshly minted sets in hopes of finding the next big discovery. This shift reflects the democratization of error coin collecting, making it more accessible to a broader audience.

COIN TYPE	POPULAR ERRORS	MARKET VALUE RANGE (APPROX.)
State Quarters (1999-2008)	Clad Layer Errors, Double Dies	$50 - $1,200
Presidential Dollars	Edge Lettering Errors, Missing Letters	$100 - $800
Commemorative Issues	Off-Center Strikes, Die Cracks	$75 - $1,500

Fluctuations in Error Coin Values

The value of error coins is highly influenced by market trends, collector demand, and economic factors. In recent years, prices for some of the most iconic error coins have risen significantly due to increased visibility and media attention. For instance, coins featured in auctions or highlighted by prominent numismatic publications often experience spikes in value as demand increases.

However, the market for error coins is not always predictable. Values can fluctuate based on factors such as economic stability, changes in collector demographics, and the availability of certain coins. When a previously unknown hoard of error coins surfaces, for example, the influx can temporarily lower prices as supply increases. Conversely, if a particular error becomes scarce or gains widespread recognition, its value can rise dramatically.

The graph below shows the average value trend for key error coins over the past decade. It highlights the impact of increased publicity and the growing interest in error coins as investments.

(Placeholder for an actual graph depicting fluctuations and trends in error coin market values over the last decade.)

Impact of Grading and Certification

Professional grading and certification services have always played a role in the value of error coins, but their importance has grown in recent years. As more collectors enter the market, the demand for certified coins—those authenticated and graded by reputable organizations like PCGS (Professional Coin Grading Service) or NGC (Numismatic Guaranty Corporation)—continues to rise. Certified error coins generally command higher prices because buyers are confident in their authenticity and condition.

Grading services also provide coins with protective slabs that preserve their state, making them more appealing to investors and serious collectors. The rise of online marketplaces has further amplified this trend, as collectors often prefer certified coins when purchasing remotely. As more collectors turn to digital platforms to buy and sell coins, the role of certification in ensuring trust and value becomes even more pronounced.

ERROR TYPE	CERTIFIED VALUE INCREASE (APPROX.)	UNCERTIFIED VALUE
Doubled Dies	25-50% higher when certified	$500 - $10,000
Off-Center Strikes	30-40% higher when certified	$100 - $1,500
Planchet Errors	20-35% higher when certified	$50 - $800

The Role of Social Media and Online Marketplaces

The influence of social media and online marketplaces on the future of error coin collecting cannot be understated. Platforms like eBay, Heritage Auctions, and specialized numismatic sites have expanded access to error coins, connecting buyers and sellers from around the world. Social media platforms like Facebook, Instagram, and Reddit have also become hubs for numismatists to share finds, discuss market trends, and build communities.

Online Auctions and Marketplaces

Online auctions and marketplaces provide opportunities for collectors to access error coins that might not be available locally. eBay remains a popular platform where collectors can bid on error coins ranging from minor anomalies to highly sought-after pieces like the 1955 Doubled Die. The accessibility of these platforms has broadened the market, allowing collectors at all levels to participate in buying and selling error coins.

The downside, however, is that online marketplaces also present challenges in terms of authenticity and trust. This is where certification becomes vital, as many buyers are unwilling to risk purchasing uncertified coins that could be misrepresented or counterfeit. The rise of online platforms has thus gone hand in hand with the growing demand for professional grading services.

Social Media and the Growth of Coin Communities

Social media's role in the future of error coin collecting is significant. Platforms like Instagram and Facebook have made it possible for collectors to showcase their finds, share information, and connect with others who share their passion. Coin enthusiasts create dedicated groups where they post images of their discoveries, seek advice, and discuss the latest trends in the error coin market.

These online communities foster collaboration and information sharing, making it easier for both new and experienced collectors to learn from each other. They also amplify the excitement surrounding error coin collecting, as posts about rare finds often go viral, sparking renewed interest and driving demand.

The Future of Error Coin Collecting

The future of error coin collecting will be shaped by the convergence of technology, market dynamics, and the numismatic community's adaptability. As technology continues to evolve, collectors will have even more tools at their disposal for identifying and authenticating coins. AI-powered apps and machine learning algorithms will likely become standard, making the hobby accessible to a broader audience while improving the precision of error detection.

Market trends will continue to influence which coins are most valuable, with modern errors gaining ground alongside classic pieces. As the market adapts to the increasing demand for certified and graded coins, the role of professional grading services will become more essential, ensuring trust in a growing digital marketplace.

Social media and online platforms will remain powerful forces in shaping collector communities and market values. The visibility and connectivity these platforms provide will likely lead to a more interactive and collaborative future for numismatics, where error coin collecting becomes a widely shared passion across generations.

As collectors navigate these trends, those who stay informed and adapt to new technologies will find themselves well-positioned to build valuable, diverse collections that stand the test of time.

CHAPTER 10
FAQS AND COMMON MYTHS ABOUT ERROR COINS

■ ■ ■ ■ ■ ■ ■ ■ ■ ■ ■ ■ ■ ■ ■ ■

Error coins have long fascinated collectors, not just because of their rarity and value, but also due to the mystery and misconceptions that often surround them. This chapter addresses some of the most frequently asked questions about error coins and debunks common myths, providing clarity and practical knowledge for both novice and experienced collectors. Understanding these questions and myths is essential for anyone looking to navigate the complex world of error coin collecting with confidence.

Addressing Frequent Questions

1. What is an error coin, and how does it differ from a variety?

An error coin is the result of a mistake during the minting process that creates an unintended anomaly. These errors can include off-center strikes, double dies, die breaks, and planchet flaws. In contrast, a variety refers to a coin that was intentionally or consistently modified during its production run, such as a change in design or mintmark placement. While both error coins and varieties are collectible, errors are generally more valued for their unexpected nature.

2. How are error coins made?

Error coins are produced when something goes wrong in the minting process. This can happen at various stages: during the preparation of the die (e.g., a doubled die), the striking process (e.g., an off-center strike), or even before the coin is struck (e.g., a planchet flaw). Each type of error provides a glimpse into the production techniques and quality control measures of the mint at that time.

3. Are all error coins valuable?

Not all error coins are valuable; their worth depends on factors like rarity, visibility of the error, and condition. Common errors, like minor die breaks or small off-center strikes, may only be worth a few dollars, while significant errors such as the 1955 Doubled Die Lincoln Cent can command thousands of dollars, especially if they are in high-grade condition.

4. How can I tell if a coin is an error or just damaged?

Distinguishing an error coin from a damaged one requires knowledge and careful examination. Errors are created during the minting process and often display specific patterns, like doubling or missing design elements, that are consistent with known types of errors. Damage, on the other hand, occurs after a coin leaves the mint and often shows irregular, random signs like scratches, dents, or bends. Using a digital microscope or consulting a professional grader can help verify the authenticity of an error.

5. Do modern coins have errors too, or is it only older coins?

Modern coins can and do have errors. In fact, advances in technology have led to different types of errors, such as edge lettering mistakes on presidential dollars or clad layer errors on state quarters. The U.S. Mint's high-speed, automated production processes mean that mistakes are still possible, although they are less frequent than in earlier periods. Collectors of modern errors often find anomalies in freshly minted coin rolls or commemorative issues.

6. Are error coins a good investment?

Error coins can be a good investment if approached with caution and knowledge. Significant and rare errors, particularly those that are iconic or have historical significance, tend to appreciate in value over time. However, like any collectible market, the value of error coins can fluctuate based on collector demand and market trends. Investing in graded and authenticated error coins from reputable services like PCGS or NGC can offer some protection and assurance of authenticity.

7. How should I store and preserve error coins to maintain their value?

Error coins should be handled carefully and stored in a controlled environment to prevent damage. Handling coins by their edges and using gloves can reduce the risk of tarnishing or scratching. For long-term storage, placing coins in holders made of archival-safe materials or in protective slabs provided by grading services is recommended. Storing them in a cool, dry place away from sunlight and humidity helps preserve their condition.

8. What is a doubled die error, and why is it so popular?

A doubled die error occurs when a die receives two misaligned impressions during its creation, resulting in the design being duplicated on the coin. This duplication is most visible on the date and inscriptions. Doubled dies are highly sought after because they are dramatic and easily identifiable. Examples like the 1955 Lincoln Cent and the 1972 Lincoln Cent are iconic pieces in the numismatic community and often fetch high prices.

9. Why are some error coins more valuable than others?

The value of an error coin depends on its rarity, the severity and visibility of the error, its condition, and collector demand. Errors that are dramatic, like the three-legged buffalo on the 1937-D Buffalo Nickel, or those that occur on coins from specific historical periods, tend to be more valuable. Minor or common errors, such as small die cracks or slight misalignments, are generally less valuable.

10. Should I have my error coin professionally graded?

Having an error coin professionally graded by services like PCGS or NGC can increase its value, especially if the coin is rare and in good condition. Grading provides authentication, an official grade, and encapsulation in a protective holder, all of which add credibility and appeal to potential buyers. However, grading services come with fees, so it's advisable to assess whether the potential increase in value justifies the cost.

Busting Myths and Misconceptions

11. Myth: All error coins are rare and worth a lot of money.

Reality: While some error coins are indeed rare and valuable, not all errors hold significant value. Common errors, such as minor off-center strikes or small die cracks, are relatively easy to find and may only be worth a few dollars. The rarity, visibility, and condition of the error largely determine its value.

12. Myth: An error coin that looks unusual is always valuable.

Reality: Not all unusual-looking coins are valuable errors. Coins that have been damaged post-mint, either by mishandling or environmental factors, may appear odd but lack value as they are not genuine errors. It's important to verify whether the anomaly occurred during the minting process or afterward.

13. Myth: It's impossible to find valuable error coins in circulation today.

Reality: Although it's rare, valuable error coins can still be found in circulation, especially modern errors like misaligned edge lettering on dollar coins or double-struck state quarters. Collectors often search coin rolls from banks or examine their pocket change for anomalies. The thrill of finding a valuable error coin is part of what keeps the hobby alive.

14. Myth: Error coins always come from older minting processes.

Reality: While older coins feature errors due to manual minting techniques, modern coins can have errors too. Technological advancements have reduced the frequency of errors, but the high-speed, automated processes used today still lead to mistakes. Modern errors, like those found on state quarters and commemorative issues, demonstrate that errors remain a part of the minting process.

15. **Myth: All error coins must be perfectly preserved to be valuable.**

Reality: While condition plays a significant role in a coin's value, some error coins can still be valuable even if they have seen circulation. For example, the 1955 Doubled Die Lincoln Cent is valuable in various conditions, and even heavily circulated examples can fetch high prices. However, uncirculated examples typically command the highest premiums.

16. **Myth: Coins that are slightly off-center are always error coins.**

Reality: Not every off-center appearance indicates an error. To qualify as a true error, a coin must show a significant portion of the design missing or misaligned due to the striking process. Minor misalignments, often less than 10% off-center, may not add significant value. Collectors seek coins where the error is more dramatic and the date is still visible.

17. **Myth: Error coins are always mistakes.**

Reality: While most error coins result from unintentional mistakes, some are created intentionally as part of mint practices. For example, the 2004 Wisconsin State Quarter with the extra leaf is speculated by some to have been an intentional modification by a mint worker. These "intentional errors" add another layer of intrigue to the numismatic world.

18. **Myth: Grading is not necessary for error coins; the error speaks for itself.**

Reality: Professional grading and certification can significantly enhance an error coin's value by verifying its authenticity and condition. A certified coin encapsulated in a slab is generally more attractive to buyers, especially in online markets where buyers cannot physically inspect the coin.

19. Myth: All doubling on coins is a valuable doubled die error.

Reality: Not all doubling is the result of a doubled die. Some coins exhibit "machine doubling" or "strike doubling," which is a mechanical flaw that occurs when the die shifts slightly during the strike. Unlike true doubled die errors, machine doubling is common and typically does not add value.

20. Myth: Coins without mintmarks are always error coins.

Reality: While some coins without mintmarks, like the 1922 "No D" Lincoln Cent, are valuable errors, not all mintmark omissions indicate an error. Some coins, especially those from Philadelphia, do not carry a mintmark as part of standard minting practice.

Understanding the facts and debunking myths is essential for navigating the world of error coin collecting. By familiarizing yourself with common questions and misconceptions, you can make informed decisions, identify genuine errors, and build a collection that not only has value but also tells the rich story of U.S. minting history. As with any hobby, knowledge is the key to success, and a well-informed collector is always in the best position to spot opportunities and avoid pitfalls.

CONCLUSION

■ ■ ■ ■ ■ ■ ■ ■ ■ ■ ■ ■ ■ ■ ■ ■

Error coin collecting is a captivating and rewarding pursuit, blending history, art, and the thrill of discovery. Whether you're a seasoned numismatist or just beginning, the world of error coins offers endless opportunities for exploration and learning. This chapter serves as an encouragement for new collectors and provides a thoughtful reflection on the evolving landscape and future of error coin collecting.

Starting a collection can feel overwhelming when faced with the vast array of coins and errors to learn about, but every great collection begins with a single coin. The journey of building that collection is as valuable as the coins themselves. The beauty of error coin collecting lies in its diversity, welcoming everyone, regardless of experience or budget.

For those new to the field, the key is to start small and grow knowledge over time. Rare or expensive pieces are not necessary at the outset; instead, focus on common errors that are accessible and affordable. Coins with off-center strikes, die cracks, and clipped planchets are excellent starting points. These simpler errors allow beginners to understand the mechanics of minting mistakes without requiring a large financial investment. As collectors become familiar with these, they develop skills to identify and appreciate more complex and valuable pieces.

The community aspect of coin collecting is just as important as building the collection itself. Error coin collecting is not a solitary pursuit; it's a shared passion that brings together people from all walks of life. Engaging with others—through local coin clubs, online forums, or social media groups—opens up opportunities to learn, trade, and grow. The collective knowledge of the numismatic community is an invaluable resource, and seasoned collectors are often eager to share their expertise. Attending coin shows, joining discussions, and participating in seminars provide new collectors with insights into the field and the market, helping them deepen their understanding and connection to the hobby.

Patience is essential. Building a valuable and meaningful collection takes time. The thrill of the hunt, the excitement of finding a new piece, and the satisfaction of expanding one's knowledge are all part of what makes error coin collecting such a rewarding experience. It's not about acquiring the most valuable coins quickly; it's about appreciating the process and the stories each coin tells.

Error coin collecting is a hobby accessible to anyone with curiosity and a willingness to learn. Even a small investment of time and effort can yield knowledge and enjoyment. The journey of discovery, whether finding an error in pocket change or acquiring a rare piece at an auction, contributes to personal growth as a collector.

The landscape of error coin collecting is dynamic, shaped by new discoveries, market trends, and technological advancements. While traditional methods of collecting still hold their charm, the future is increasingly intertwined with technology, expanding the ways collectors engage and build their collections.

Technology is transforming how error coins are found and authenticated. Digital microscopes, high-resolution imaging devices, and AI-powered detection tools allow for more precise identification. These tools, once reserved for professionals, are now available to hobbyists, democratizing the hobby and enabling new collectors to develop expertise with greater confidence. Digital platforms are also revolutionizing how collectors buy, sell, and trade coins. Online marketplaces and auction sites provide global access, while mobile apps offer real-time insights into coin values and error types, integrating augmented reality and AI for an interactive experience. These innovations make error coin collecting more engaging and accessible, particularly for younger generations.

As technology advances, the future may include even more sophisticated applications like blockchain for tracking provenance, ensuring authenticity, and establishing a verifiable history for each coin. Further development of AI-powered grading systems may also become standard, providing consistent and accurate assessments that minimize human error. These innovations will enhance the hobby, offering new tools and resources that support collectors in building their expertise and expanding their collections.

Market trends are evolving alongside technological advances. While classic error coins like the 1955 Doubled Die Lincoln Cent or the 1937-D Three-Legged Buffalo Nickel will always hold prestige, there is growing interest in modern errors. Coins from the state quarter series, presidential dollars, and recent commemorative issues are gaining attention as collectors recognize the value of anomalies in contemporary minting processes. This shift indicates a broader market where collectors are seeking not just historical pieces but also looking ahead to identify future discoveries and opportunities.

Modern errors, accessible in circulation or through coin rolls, make the hobby more approachable for newcomers. This availability encourages a new generation of collectors to participate, using coins they encounter daily as entry points into the world of error collecting. This democratization keeps the market vibrant, as fresh interest and new perspectives continue to energize the field.

Globalization is also playing a significant role. With online platforms and marketplaces, numismatics is no longer bound by regional or national limits. Collectors now access coins from around the world, expanding the scope of error coin collecting beyond U.S. borders. This global approach offers insights into minting processes and errors in different countries, adding diversity to collections. Collectors who embrace this broader perspective gain exposure to a wider range of errors and stories, enriching their collections and understanding of the numismatic world.

The expansion of networks through social media and online communities is shaping the future. Platforms like Instagram, Facebook, and Reddit create vibrant spaces where collectors showcase their finds, share knowledge, and engage with others on the latest trends. This connectivity makes the hobby more interactive and accessible, amplifying the excitement of error coin collecting as posts about rare finds often gain widespread attention and drive market demand.

For error coin collecting to remain sustainable and thriving, the numismatic community must continue supporting education and promoting responsible practices. Many coin clubs, grading organizations, and societies offer resources and seminars that educate collectors about errors, grading, and the history of minting. These efforts help ensure that new generations of collectors are well-informed, prepared to engage meaningfully, and equipped to maintain the hobby's vibrancy.

Sustainability also involves encouraging ethical practices, such as proper coin preservation and respecting each piece's historical significance. By fostering a culture of learning and appreciation, the community can ensure that error coin collecting remains vibrant and engaging for years to come.

Looking ahead, the future of error coin collecting is bright. The hobby offers endless possibilities for discovery, learning, and personal growth. Technological innovations, expanding global networks, and a dynamic market ensure that the hobby will continue to evolve, offering collectors new ways to engage with coins and connect with each other.

For new collectors, embracing the available resources—ranging from traditional coin clubs to digital tools and online communities—will build expertise and create a rich collecting experience. The market will likely expand further, and those who are curious, patient, and knowledgeable will find themselves well-positioned to benefit from these changes.

For experienced collectors, the future offers opportunities to deepen their collections, discover new areas of interest, and share their expertise with the growing community. The evolution of the hobby presents new challenges and opportunities, ensuring that there is always something fresh to learn and explore.

Error coin collecting is a field with a rich past and an exciting future. It is a journey that offers not only material rewards but also a deeper understanding of history, minting processes, and the human touch behind every coin. Whether you are new to collecting or a seasoned expert, the world of error coins invites you to explore, connect, and grow. Embrace the opportunities, engage with the community, and watch as your passion for collecting—and your collection itself—thrives.

Appendix

The appendix provides additional information and resources for collectors to deepen their understanding of error coins, enhance their collecting journey, and make informed decisions in the marketplace. This section includes a glossary of essential terms, recommended resources, market tables, and lists of notable error coins to guide collectors in expanding their collections.

Glossary

1. Doubled Die

An error that occurs when the die is struck twice with misalignment, causing a doubled image on the coin's surface. This is one of the most sought-after types of errors due to its dramatic visual impact.

2. Off-Center Strike

A coin struck outside its center, resulting in a portion of the design missing. The degree of off-centering can vary, and collectors value examples that display the date and other key features clearly.

3. Planchet

The blank metal disc from which a coin is made. Planchet errors occur when there are flaws in this disc, such as missing pieces (clipped planchets) or improper thickness.

4. Die Crack

A small, visible crack on the coin's surface caused by a break in the die used to strike the coin. These errors create raised lines on the coin and can increase its value depending on the severity and visibility.

5. Mintmark

A small letter on a coin indicating where it was minted (e.g., "D" for Denver, "S" for San Francisco). Errors can occur when mintmarks are missing, doubled, or misaligned.

6. Edge Lettering

The inscriptions on the edge of some coins, such as presidential dollars. Errors include missing or misaligned edge lettering, which can increase the value of these modern coins.

7. Lamination Error

A defect caused by impurities or foreign material in the coin's metal. This results in peeling or flaking on the coin's surface, making it more desirable to collectors.

8. Machine Doubling

A common issue where the die shifts slightly during the strike, causing a shallow doubling effect. Unlike true doubled die errors, machine doubling does not typically add significant value.

9. Clad Layer Error

An error involving the outer layer of modern coins, typically resulting in missing or partial layers that reveal the core metal underneath.

This type of error is more common in state quarters and other modern coinage.

10. Die Clash

An error that occurs when the obverse and reverse dies collide without a planchet between them, leaving traces of each die's design on the opposite side of the coin.

Resources for Collectors

Books and Guides:

- *The Official Red Book: A Guide Book of United States Coins* – A comprehensive resource for coin collectors, featuring prices, coin specifications, and historical information.
- *Strike It Rich with Pocket Change* by Ken Potter and Brian Allen – Focuses specifically on error coins and the potential to find valuable pieces in circulation.
- *Cherrypickers' Guide to Rare Die Varieties of United States Coins* by Bill Fivaz and J.T. Stanton – An essential reference for those interested in identifying rare error coins and die varieties.

Websites:

- **PCGS (Professional Coin Grading Service)** – Offers resources on coin grading, authentication, and pricing trends. Provides access to certified coin values and auction results.
- **NGC (Numismatic Guaranty Corporation)** – Another leading grading service that offers online tools, resources, and educational articles for coin collectors.
- **Coin Community Forum** – An online community where collectors discuss their finds, seek advice, and learn from fellow numismatists.

Apps:

- **Coinoscope** – A mobile app that allows users to identify coins by taking a picture. It's useful for collectors who want quick information on errors or coin values.
- **NGC Coin Collecting App** – Provides access to certification information, market trends, and pricing guides, making it a valuable tool for collectors on the go.

Market Tables

Below are tables displaying approximate market values for some of the most popular error coins. These values are averages based on recent auction results and collector markets; actual prices may vary depending on condition, certification, and demand.

ERROR COIN	CON- DI- TION	MARKET VALUE RANGE (USD)
1955 Doubled Die Lincoln Cent	Circu- lated	$1,000 - $2,500
	Mint State	$10,000 - $15,000+
1937-D Three-Legged Buffalo	Circu- lated	$500 - $2,000
	Mint State	$25,000 - $50,000+
1942/41 Mercury Dime (Phila- delphia)	Very Fine	$1,500 - $3,000
	Mint State	$12,000 - $18,000

2004 Wisconsin Extra Leaf Quarter	MS-63	$250 - $500
	MS-66	$1,000 - $1,500
1922 No D Lincoln Cent	Circulated	$500 - $1,500
	Mint State	$20,000 - $30,000+

MODERN ERROR COIN	ERROR TYPE	MARKET VALUE RANGE (USD)
Presidential Dollar	Edge Lettering Error	$100 - $800
State Quarter (2004 Wisconsin)	Extra Leaf (High/Low)	$200 - $1,200
Lincoln Cent (2009-2022)	Clad Layer Error	$50 - $500

Notable Error Coin Lists

Top U.S. Error Coins to Look For:

- **1955 Doubled Die Lincoln Cent**: A classic and highly desirable error, known for its dramatic doubling effect.
- **1937-D Three-Legged Buffalo Nickel**: An iconic error resulting from over-polishing, creating the illusion of a three-legged buffalo.
- **1922 No D Lincoln Cent**: A significant mintmark error from the Denver Mint where the "D" was missing due to a grease-filled die.
- **1942/41 Mercury Dime**: A rare overdate error where the "1941" was struck over by the "1942" die, leaving remnants of the earlier date visible.

- **2004 Wisconsin State Quarter (Extra Leaf)**: Modern errors like the "extra leaf" (high and low) on the corn stalk make these quarters highly sought after.
- **1999 Wide "AM" Lincoln Cent**: A variety where the "A" and "M" in "AMERICA" are spaced further apart than usual, appearing in early proof dies used for business strikes.

Modern Errors That Are Increasing in Value:

- **Presidential Dollars (Missing Edge Lettering)**: Coins missing their edge inscriptions have become popular and valuable among modern collectors.
- **Sacagawea Dollars (2000-P Cheerios Dollar)**: These coins, distributed in early 2000 with Cheerios boxes, feature enhanced details and are considered valuable.
- **2007 John Adams Dollar (Doubled Edge Lettering)**: An error where the edge lettering was doubled, creating a distinct appearance.

Summary

The appendix serves as a quick reference for collectors, providing essential terms, recommended resources, and market information. Understanding the glossary helps clarify the technicalities of error coins, while the resources and market tables provide tools for expanding knowledge and making informed buying and selling decisions. The error coin lists highlight the most notable pieces to look for, whether focusing on classic errors or modern anomalies. Together, these elements enhance the collecting experience and guide enthusiasts toward building valuable and engaging error coin collections.

YOU EXCLUSIVE BONUS
■ ■ ■ ■ ■ ■ ■ ■ ■ ■ ■ ■ ■ ■ ■

SCAN THE QR-CODE BELOW TO GET YOU EXCLUSIVE BONUS!

Made in the USA
Las Vegas, NV
16 November 2024

11931349R00085